Preventing Miscarriage

Also by Jonathan Scher, M.D., and Carol Dix
Everything You Need to Know About Pregnancy

Preventing Miscarriage

THE GOOD NEWS

Jonathan Scher, M.D.
Carol Dix

HARPER & ROW, PUBLISHERS, New York
Grand Rapids, Philadelphia, St. Louis, San Francisco
London, Singapore, Sydney, Tokyo, Toronto

1817

FIRST EDITION

Designed by Alma Orenstein

Library of Congress Cataloging-in-Publication Data

Scher, Jonathan.
    Preventing miscarriage: the good news/Jonathan Scher, Carol Dix.
        p. cm.
    ISBN 0-06-016137-X
    1. Miscarriage—Prevention—Popular works. I. Dix, Carol.
    II. Title.
    RG648.S34   1990
    618.3'92—dc20   89-45063

---

90 91 92 93 94 CC/HC 10 9 8 7 6 5 4 3 2 1

This book is dedicated to my wife, Brenda, and my daughters, Amanda and Robyn, for their support and encouragement; and to my patients, who inspired me to write it.

Contents

PART THREE

Are You Ready to Try Again?

List of Illustrations

Acknowledgments

I would like to thank my colleagues Drs. Sami David, Susan Cowchock, Jacob Rand, Vincent Brandeis, Hugh Melnick, and Victor Reyniak. They helped me in the management of patients and taught me about miscarriages.

My thanks also to my partners Drs. Thomas Kerenyi and Victor Grazi for their help and advice in caring for our patients; to our compassionate nurses, Karen Herbster, Kathy Burke, Fran Petinos, Jane King, and Pat Prinz; to Mary Duffy, our wonderful medical technician, for her help with all the testing; and to Terry Karten, my editor at Harper and Row, for being meticulous and patient.

Thanks to Paula Koz for all her help with the illustrations.

Preface

My interest and involvement in the field of recurrent miscarriage began about fifteen years ago. It was obvious to me, as a busy obstetrician working in New York City, endeavoring to keep up with the latest research and methodology, that great advances were being made in my field. Obstetrics was becoming more of a science and, perhaps, less of an art. But what I continued to find upsetting was that couples who miscarried, who lost a pregnancy, were really still being ignored by medical professionals.

Moreover, society at large, including doctors and nurses, had no accepted ritual for couples who had suffered pregnancy loss. Often the grieving mother and father were sent home from the hospital—empty armed—to feel the full extent of their loss when they found themselves alone again at home, isolated by their grief. They had each other to lean on, but there was little sympathy forthcoming, and no opportunities to deal with that grief even from family and friends, let alone professionals.

Doctors were hampered by the lack of medical answers as to why many miscarriages occurred. They were also frustrated by the lack of information about the early stages of pregnancy (particularly about the first twelve weeks, known as the "first trimester"). This lack of knowledge either resulted in no treatment being offered, or in inappropriate treatment being given out of desperation to do something. Patients tended to go from doctor to doctor, having various tests done in a random fashion, without much coordination.

But it was also becoming obvious to me that many of these couples wanted to talk, to express feelings about their loss. They found it difficult to grieve over something they could not visualize (most likely, they had not seen the fetus because ultrasound only recently became common). Many also felt responsible for causing the miscarriage—self-guilt and blame were common emotions—though in the majority of cases that guilt was without foundation.

Eventually, I started a clinic at Mount Sinai Hospital, in New York City, where we treated women who had undergone recurrent miscarriages. The Pregnancy Support Clinic was staffed by physicians, nurses, and social workers. Besides the best we could offer in medical intervention, the women and their partners were offered emotional support, and a hot line was established so that patients could call whenever they felt anxious about certain symptoms.

The positive results in terms of live full-term births showed that patients responded well to this rational, orderly approach to their problem; and they also appreciated the reassurance offered by concerned professionals.

The good news resulting from the establishment of special clinics, plus further research and new technological developments, is that more and more causes of miscarriage are now being discovered, and appropriate treatments are being offered. Significantly, the psychological consequences of miscarriage are being appreciated and studied. Couples can now feel confident that their pregnancies are being managed by dedicated doctors, nurses, and social workers, and that if a miscarriage does happen, the same care will be put into action after a loss.

The message of *Preventing Miscarriage* is that, in these days of good contraception, postponement of childbearing, and the planning of smaller families, doctors will now be prepared to investigate a miscarriage—in some cases, under very special circumstances, even your first. You do not always have to undergo three or more such losses before your problem is appreciated and treated.

If you are reading this book, maybe you are still grieving the loss of a child. I want to emphasize that both Carol Dix, my coauthor, and I are sensitive to your feelings, which is why we want to pass on to you some of the new optimism. Many of the women's stories that you will be reading in these pages tell of years of despair and feelings of failure; of battles with disappointment; of the point where they nearly gave up all hope. Then, by being exposed to new areas of investigation into the causes of miscarriage and to new treatments, they now have beautiful, normal, healthy babies in their nurseries back home.

Their stories are full of courage, a tremendous fighting spirit, and a determination to bring the reproductive cycle to its natural fruition. We hope that these stories, coupled with the most up-to-date research in an ever-changing world of medical information, will help boost your spirits, too. You will be reading in this book about the very newest developments in medical science for the prevention of recurrent miscarriages, the results of which are only now being appreciated. For doctors, as well as for the couples involved, this is all very exciting.

Miscarriage need no longer be a soul-wrenching mystery to you and your partner. It need no longer remain a source of chronic depression, feelings of inadequacy or failure, or a bottomless pit of lonely pain. There really is hope and a strong direction for the future for most couples.

JONATHAN SCHER, M.D.

PART ONE

Miscarriage and You

1

"You Don't Ever Forget a Miscarriage"

D EBBIE has a four-year-old daughter. Since that birth, she has lost three babies through miscarriages. Right now, she is at the 15-week stage of another pregnancy and is finally being treated with one of the newer methods for miscarriage prevention. Although anxiety-ridden, she says she is praying hard.

I don't see how you can be expected to "forget" a miscarriage. Even if it happened at only 8 weeks, there had been a baby inside you. There was hope, and planning, and dreams. We don't let each other grieve the right way. It's not "just a miscarriage," but a *baby* that has been lost. Whether you know someone for ten years, or it's a baby that's only been inside of you a few weeks, there's still a relationship there that you have made. It's become part of your life.

All the time, women like me hear that "it's God's way" or "it was meant to be." But those words don't take away the pain, even if they're right. If you want to talk about it at all, friends, relatives, they try and change the subject, and you'll be asked, "Do you want a cup of tea or coffee?" What I say is, if it was really God's will then why does He let me get pregnant so easily?

If a friend of yours died, people wouldn't say, "Oh, it was God's way," and if you're crying over that death, they wouldn't say, "Stop crying." I've found that the only people who really understand what I'm going through are others who've undergone miscarriages; they can share their sense of loss with you.

I was really strong for the first miscarriage. But by this third one, I've just been thrown. How strong can you be? I hold on for my husband's and my daughter's sakes. But I cry when I'm alone in the evenings. It's something I'll never forget.

Debbie is not a wealthy woman. Her husband works as a store manager. They can scarcely afford the medical bills involved. Yet her genuine desire for another child drives her on. She is being treated for an autoimmune disorder that has been detected as the possible cause of her problem.

Philippa, socially Debbie's opposite, is the wife of a wealthy lawyer. A graciously attractive woman, she, too, had a daughter before suffering any problems with miscarriages. That daughter is now eleven years old; in the years since her birth Philippa has lost five more babies. Recently, Philippa experienced another devastating loss, another miscarriage. At the age of forty-two, both she and her husband feel that they have lost control over this vital area of their lives.

"No One Knows How to Respond to You"

There are people for whom life always goes easily. Until I was thirty, I was one of those people. Then, after that first miscarriage, I realized I had passed through a door onto the other side, a magic door. Now I'm with all those people who suffer, who grieve, who cannot make life run along the lines they'd prefer.

Once you've gone through that door, most people just don't know how to respond to you. I can't really blame them; until it happened to me I wouldn't have known either. But I've had friends cross the street rather than have to confront me. Most people, I think, would prefer to pretend the baby never happened, rather than talk about your loss with you.

After the loss of this latest baby—a little girl, born at 23 weeks—my husband took me away for a vacation to Barbados. It was lucky we were staying at a very proper English resort, because the one thing I didn't want was anyone becoming too close and friendly. How do you answer the common question, "How many children do you have?" What I want to say to them is something along the lines of "I have one live child and a garden full of babies we have buried." But you can't do that to your random well-wisher, can you? I'm not strong enough yet to take such a stance.

On the way back from that vacation, the movie on the plane unexpectedly showed a scene of a woman giving birth. That was the last thing I wanted to see. But it was a jammed flight and I couldn't get out of my seat. I took the headphones off so I wouldn't have to listen. But I burst into tears. There I was still postmiscarriage, bleeding heavily, and my milk started to gush forth. I was wet and crying uncontrollably. The woman sitting next to me tried to move as far away as she could get. But the stewardess kindly brought me a blanket to cover myself.

You go through all the same hormonal and emotional changes as after a full-term birth. And you can't explain your situation to anyone. Would anyone have wanted to hear?

For some women the loss of a baby may be almost unnoticed. Happening in the very early weeks following conception, the blood loss often appears like a heavy but late period. To other women, the loss is traumatic, painful, and most deeply experienced. Today, the medical and caring professions are becoming aware that no woman should be ignored at the time of such loss. If the woman was emotionally involved with the pregnancy, then the miscarriage should be seen as an important time in her life, and in that of the couple. No one, neither the woman nor her partner, should be left rocking herself or himself to sleep at night, vexed with unanswered questions such as: Why did this happen to me? What is wrong with us that we cannot produce a baby? Why has such sadness been thrust upon us? Can we be sure it won't happen again? Could we possibly bear the pain of going through the excitement, and the hope, of another pregnancy only to suffer this devastating loss one more time?

An early miscarriage may be a very normal, natural way for nature to abort a deformed or unhealthy embryo; or it may be a sign of some very real cause as to why some pregnancies will not hold and go to term. So let us now turn to some questions that are most often asked by women and their partners when they have miscarried.

What Is the Actual Definition of a Miscarriage?

The term *miscarriage* (which may also be referred to by your doctor as *spontaneous abortion*) actually refers these days to the loss of a pregnancy up to the end of the 20th week. This is now an accepted working definition in the medical literature. Until quite recently, 26 or 28 weeks were seen as the overall range for a "miscarriage," but modern science and recent achievements in technology have led to major changes in the definition.

We used to define a miscarriage as the loss of a pregnancy before 28 weeks because, until recently, no baby born before that time could survive, and a less-than-28-week-old fetus, therefore, could not be regarded as viable. Now, we are able in certain cases to save babies born at 26 weeks—and there have been rare cases of even younger babies surviving to normal life—so the cut off point has been pushed back to 20 weeks.

That still leaves us with a twilight area for those women who lose babies between the 20th and 26th weeks—this is a time when fetal life may yet be saved—and their condition might even be termed "premature labor." Major medical advances are being made in treating babies of this age. The causes for any loss between the 20th and 26th weeks should still be investigated so that we can find out just what happened in order to prevent a recurrence.

Can the Baby's Weight Be a Definition?

There has been some discussion in the medical literature as to whether the baby's weight would provide a better definition. For example, could the lost embryo or fetus that weighs 500 grams or less be defined as a "miscarriage?" But this approach is faulty since at 20 weeks a baby may weigh 300, 500, or 600 grams. What is most important is how long the baby has been *in the uterus* and its level of physical development.

There has been one documented case of an infant who survived for at least a year, after being born two months early, at a weight of 397 grams; that means the baby was born at 32 weeks weighing just one pound, instead of the expected three to four pounds. This baby was *not* in fact premature at 32 weeks but was "growth-retarded"—a clear distinction—because the fetus was too low in weight for its age.

To use one other example, if you give birth to a 5 ½-pound baby at 36 weeks, that baby might suffer from lung disease. Ironically, if you smoked heavily or had high blood pressure, and gave birth to a 5-pound baby at full term (40 weeks), the baby would have the better chance of survival—simply because it would have been alive in the uterus longer and its organs would have developed further. So you can see that the weight of a baby alone does not always tell the full story.

Although many couples these days pray that premature labor around 24 to 26 weeks will indeed mean a live baby—one who can be nurtured and kept alive in a hospital's neonatal intensive care unit—tragedy sometimes results from such a situation. In chapter 8, we will return to the story of Philippa. She and her husband have run the gamut of experiences, including premature labor at 26 weeks with a baby born alive—and hopefully capable of independent life. As Philippa describes so eloquently, the human cost, in emotional, financial, and spiritual terms, can be catastrophic.

Just How Often Do Miscarriages Happen?

Whether the statistic is one in ten or one in a hundred thousand, when it happens to *you* the incidence seems irrevelant. To you, it's one hundred percent. Nevertheless, because we know so little about miscarriages and the real number of occurrences, most people ask this question.

The answer, unfortunately, is that no one knows for certain. Every scientific article that comes out, every magazine article, offers a different statistic.

What we do know is that every day many more miscarriages happen than we record, because some may appear as just a heavy period (and women who use intrauterine devices, IUDs, for contraception may be miscarrying when they assume they are having a period).

In general, we can now accept that from 50 to 60 percent of first pregnancies miscarry, and the figure may in reality be higher. This means that at least one in two first pregnancies are lost naturally. Just last year, however, the *New England Journal of Medicine* came out with the controversial figure of 31 percent for all "implanting" embryos (the ones that have actually embedded in the uterus) that miscarry. As many as 75 percent of all fertilized eggs, including those that never implant, do not yield a full-term baby.

Of diagnosed pregnancies, however, where the woman knows she is pregnant, the rate is reassuringly lower—about 10 to 20 percent will end in miscarriage.

About one in four women, in a group aged 20 to 40, confessed to having had a miscarriage, and one in three hundred had suffered three or more miscarriages.

Advanced maternal age is a known cause of miscarriages, and this is influencing the statistics since the age of women having babies is steadily increasing.

But now we are beginning to get a better idea of just how common miscarriages really are, because the new pregnancy tests can diagnose conception 6 to 7 days after the egg and sperm meet, that is, 8 to 10 days before a woman would even notice a missed period. Together with the use of ultrasound from the earliest stages of pregnancy, the new forms of technology can be very accurate.

Indeed, both ultrasound and the use of very sensitive pregnancy tests have completely altered the practice of obstetrics. Twenty years ago, before a doctor could tell a woman she was definitely pregnant she probably already knew herself! Tests in those days often did not yield results until the woman was 2 to 3 months pregnant. The patient's urine had to be injected into frogs or rabbits, which were then sacrificed and examined to diagnose pregnancy. Today, if every woman had a very early pregnancy test done, *every month,* throughout her reproductive life, then the rate of spontaneous miscarriage would probably turn out to be even higher.

The term *ultrasound* has become extremely familiar to any woman who has been pregnant. Many hospitals and doctors' offices now offer routine ultrasound scans, especially in the early weeks of pregnancy. Sonography makes use of high-frequency sound waves that cannot be heard by the human ear. They are emitted from a probe (transducer) attached to the ultrasound machine, and, as they pass through human tissue, they rebound at each surface, returning to the machine where an image is created. It is important to realize that ultrasound has nothing to do with X-rays and is not a form of radiation.

With skilled usage, ultrasound has become a great boon to the obstetrician. For example, we can now estimate a baby's maturity accurately and can therefore double-check the mother's dates. If you have a scan in the first 8 to 9 weeks of your pregnancy so that your doctor can measure the length of the baby (known as the "crown-rump" length), and if a problem arises later in the pregnancy, the doctor will have an accurate assessment of the baby's maturity upon which to work.

Why Three Miscarriages Were Once Necessary Before Investigation Occurred

The medical profession has always relied on the odds in favor of a couple having a normal, healthy pregnancy, after they have had a miscarriage, as positive proof that miscarriages can be overcome naturally. These statistics were the main reason the profession insisted a woman should have at least three recurrent miscarriages, without a live birth in between, before she would be deemed eligible for testing or for investigation into the causes. Another reason for waiting, of course, was that the causes of a miscarriage were barely known until recently.

Because the chances of a healthy live birth after a previous miscarriage were seen to be relatively high, investigation was not thought necessary until a woman had undergone three miscarriages. For example:

- After one spontaneous miscarriage, the chances for a successful pregnancy next time are almost 87 percent (or 13 percent for a miscarriage);
- After two spontaneous miscarriages, the chances for a successful pregnancy are 60 percent (or 40 percent for a miscarriage);
- After three or more spontaneous miscarriages, the chances for giving birth are 40 percent (or 60 percent for a miscarriage).

This last figure suggests that some recurrent or persistent medical cause may be operating.

Why Has Information on Miscarriages Been So Slow in Coming?

No aspect of pregnancy has received as little attention as the first trimester (three months or 12 weeks). Yet by the 12th week, the embryo has formed most of its organs (known as the period of organogenesis) and is complete. This is the most dangerous and likely time for a miscarriage. We must all appreciate that those same 12 weeks are ethically a very difficult time to investigate a pregnancy, since no tests can be performed that may harm the embryo at this critical stage of its life. And certainly there is little place for the usual scientific method to prove a cause for a miscarriage—the "double blind" trial, whereby some women are given a treatment that is thought to be effective, while a control group is not, or is given a placebo —as this may lead to withholding necessary treatment.

The earlier lack of interest in the first trimester has kept our statistics uncertain and our scientific knowledge meager. It is difficult to excuse this previous lack of knowledge of or interest in miscarriages. In fact, even standard texts include very little on the subject. Until recently, moreover, women who miscarried in the first few weeks of pregnancy were admitted to the gynecological ward of a hospital, rather than to the maternity ward. They were not appreciated as women trying to have a baby, as obstetric patients. But fortunately the situation regarding miscarriages is now changing.

Why Waiting Until Three Miscarriages Have Occurred Is Not Always Necessary

Any miscarriage is tragic. No matter how many miscarriages you have had and no matter how early in pregnancy they occurred, they are still emotionally devastating. Saying, however well meant, "Don't worry, you can try again" or "It wasn't really a baby" is now generally acknowledged to be the wrong attitude to take.

The major changes in a woman's hormonal makeup take place *early* in pregnancy, almost just after conception. Mothers undergo huge hormonal fluctuations, and we tend to think this grows along with her swelling belly. But, in fact, the greatest impact of maternal feeling occurs *early* in the pregnancy. So, when you lose a pregnancy, it does feel just like you have lost a child, an anticipated child. There is scientific (hormonal) proof that these feelings occur! At last women are being believed.

Now that we are finding treatable causes and not mere associations with miscarriage, it seems kinder to investigate women after two miscarriages, and maybe even one, rather than make them suffer through three such experiences. In about 50 percent of the cases, we can now identify a cause and offer treatment. The percentage is increasing all the time as medical knowledge improves.

There are other reasons why each pregnancy should now be viewed as premium:

- People are tending to have smaller and smaller families
- Women are delaying childbearing until a certain point in their careers
- It just does not make emotional, or even economic, sense to allow what is coldly termed "pregnancy wastage" to continue
- If a woman is 40 years old, or older, and this is her first pregnancy loss, it would be a pity not to search for a cause of the miscarriage and possibly to treat the problem. Some of the tests are simple to do and do not involve elaborate medical intervention.

"It's One Heck of a Way to Be Pregnant!"

Robert and Grace went through both in vitro fertilization and immunological treatment against miscarriage before giving birth to their son, who is now a beautiful nine month old. They have a very down-to-earth approach to the problem that dogged their lives for so many years. As Robert tells us:

When you suffer a miscarriage, or infertility, you become part of a growing underground, a subgroup of people all in the same situation, and you feel no one out there is addressing your problems. It's an extraordinarily stressful time that might go on for years. In a day and age when people are used to feeling in control of their lives, it hurts to feel so totally out of control.

Even when you do manage to get pregnant again, you daren't tell your friends or family. There's none of the normal glow and enjoyment of pregnancy. It's a very strange panicky time, very secretive. And for the man, the extra stress is in feeling he has to be emotionally tough to carry his wife's total vulnerability.

It's one heck of a way to be pregnant!

What Should You Expect from Your Doctor After a Miscarriage?

Once you and your partner have had time to overcome your grief, and to feel ready to approach another conception, then it is time to consult an obstetrician about your future.

Your doctor will ask not only about the bleeding and/or cramping that led up to the miscarriage, but also about your previous general medical and menstrual history. There will be many questions. Each question and answer may suggest its own line of treatment. For example, did you have late onset of menarche (the age of your first period) or a history of missing periods, either of which might be a sign of poor ovulation. If so, you may need an *endometrial biopsy* (see below) to test for hormonal problems. If you have a history of severe pain with your periods *(dysmenorrhea),* it might also lead your doctor to look for an abnormality in the shape of your uterus.

If you have had more than one miscarriage, is there a pattern that has emerged? If they were all in the second trimester, for example, the entrance to the uterus may be too weak to hold a pregnancy. This is called an *incompetent cervix.*

You will probably be asked about activity levels of all kinds—whether, for example, you partake in very vigorous sports. If you have been very active, you may be advised to rest more during the next pregnancy, at least until you are past the first 12 to 13 weeks, or beyond the point where you last miscarried. Similarly, you might be advised to avoid intercourse at least until the end of the first trimester.

Is there a *family* history of miscarriage on either your or your partner's side? This might suggest a familial problem. If your mother had numerous miscarriages, maybe she was given diethylstilbestrol (DES) when she was pregnant with you, which may cause you to have fertility problems or to miscarry.

Do you or your partner take drugs? Both medications and recreational drugs can be factors in causing miscarriages. Do either of you smoke or drink heavily?

As you can see, your partner's history is also relevant, and he should go to the doctor with you, at least during your first consultation.

Your medical history may include details of previous D & Cs (dilatation and curettages, also known as induced abortions) to terminate a pregnancy. Your doctor will need to know about them, especially if they were done more than five years ago when the entrance to the uterus was probably opened mechanically with metal dilators.

There is now known to be an increase in second trimester (13 to 26 weeks) miscarriages in women with a previous history of *multiple* terminated pregnancies—multiple being as many as six or seven. The reason for the miscarriages will likely be an incompetent (weak) cervix, a result of overstretching during the repeated abortions. Much of the data on the effect of repeated terminations on miscarriage has come from Eastern Europe, where abortion has long been used as a form of contraception. But, be reassured, a history of two or three early induced abortions (terminations) should not increase your risk of a miscarriage. Nevertheless, you must tell your doctor about your abortion history.

After all the questions, the doctor's physical examination usually includes a general physical checkup, to detect any medical disorders, and a pelvic examination to see if your pelvic organs are healthy and the shape of your uterus is normal. At the time of the routine pap smear, your doctor may take a sample of the cervical secretion and culture it to detect infections that, although they may be asymptomatic, could contribute to a miscarriage.

The doctor may then discuss with you and your partner the various possibilities which resulted in your problem, and a series of tests may be planned depending on your particular case.

The possible causes of a miscarriage—and tests to be done—are listed below. They will be explained in more detail later in the book.

1. *Infections.* To detect these, samples of secretions may have to be taken from the cervix, very much like a pap smear. Your partner must also be tested for infection. His samples can be taken from seminal fluid at the time of a semen analysis, which would be done at a special laboratory. Alternatively, it can be done in the doctor's office from a clean urine sample, and by passing a fine Q-Tip into his urethra at the tip of his penis. However, most men balk at this!

2. *Endocrine causes.* Your checkup may have given a clue as to some endocrine, or hormonal, cause (the words *endocrine* and *hormonal* mean the same). The doctor may order blood to be drawn from your arm to study the thyroid gland, as gross thyroid disturbances may contribute to a miscarriage. Also, in order to ensure that during your menstrual cycle you produce enough progesterone—the most important hormone in early pregnancy—the doctor may order a blood progesterone measurement in the second half of your next cycle. You may also be asked to keep a temperature chart. The rise in your temperature at the time of egg production, or ovulation—the thermal shift—indicates an adequate amount of progesterone. Ovulation occurs 14 days before a period.

The endometrial biopsy is an accurate method of determining if you are ovulating and if you are producing an adequate supply of hormones after ovulation to maintain a pregnancy. It involves taking a sample of your uterine lining, late in the menstrual cycle (around day 25 or 26 from the start of your period). The procedure does cause some short-lived cramping, for which a mild pain killer may be taken. How the biopsy is done will be explained later.

Another hormone that doctors often monitor following a miscarriage is prolactin. If this runs at a very high level, it can interfere with early pregnancy, but treatment is available.

3. *Uterine abnormalities.* If, from your history, this seems to be the cause of your miscarriage, you will be referred to a radiologist for an hysterogram to see if the uterus is normal in structure and to check for cervical incompetence—that is, to see if the cervix is too weak to hold a pregnancy. Antibiotics are often given before this procedure to prevent uterine infection from the injection of the dye. An hysterogram is an X-ray, usually done in a radiologist's office. It may cause some cramping and mild discomfort since the dye is injected into the uterus through the cervix.

4. *Genetics.* If a genetic cause is suspected, you and your partner will probably be referred to a genetics testing center where, after an interview, blood will be drawn from both your arms for chromosome testing. White cells are taken from both blood samples, and the cells are grown to see if you and your partner have normal chromosomes, which may give a clue as to why you are miscarrying.

5. *Antiphospholipid antibodies.* This new test is for a condition now thought to account for more and more miscarriages that were previously inexplicable. The test determines whether certain antibodies are present in the bloodstream. The ones of interest are: the *anticardiolipin antibody* and *cold lupus anticoagulant.* If either of these antibodies is found, treatment that does

seem to be successful is available. But, remember, this is a very new approach. Also from the blood sample, your platelets (blood factors important in clotting) can be measured—particularly if you have had more than one miscarriage. A high platelet count is another condition that can be treated.

6. *Immunology.* Another exciting avenue of research, in use already, is the detection of antibodies that *you* as the mother may be producing early in your pregnancy. Essentially, because the pregnancy consists of your partner's tissue as well as your own, your antibodies may be rejecting it, unless as normally happens, you form a protective factor in your blood. As a screening test for this condition, your blood will be tested at a special laboratory. These alloimmune problems are asymptomatic—so they should not affect you at any time other than pregnancy. A full explanation of why this happens is in chapter 5, page 127.

7. *Medical disorders.* If, at the time of your examination, you are discovered to be suffering from a medical disorder such as uncontrolled diabetes and thyroid disease, heart disease, or high blood pressure, you will be referred to your internist for treatment. It is known that some general medical disorders may contribute to miscarriages.

When Can You Try to Conceive Again Following a Miscarriage?

The decision when to start a new pregnancy lies solely with *you* as a couple. There used to be conflicting advice about whether to wait one month, three months, or even longer. But it has now been shown that there is no medical reason for waiting—other than to make sure you are emotionally and psychologically ready to begin again—unless of course you are undergoing treatment for a specific cause of your miscarriage.

When I say give yourself a chance to recover psychologically, I am also referring to the hormonal changes your body has undergone. For example, it takes one to two months for all the pregnancy hormones to leave your blood stream, which means that even three weeks or more after a complete miscarriage or a D & C, you could still have a positive pregnancy test! Usually your period returns four to six weeks after a miscarriage, and you could begin trying to conceive during that cycle if you wish. You do not have to wait.

People's emotional reactions to miscarriages vary enormously. For some, part of the reaction evolves from fear, because miscarriages tend to happen so suddenly, with pain, bleeding, and maybe some loss of tissue. There's the rush to the hospital, the mystery of the unknown cause, the grief, and finally the feeling that maybe somehow you were to blame. The fear grows into anxiety because of all the unanswered questions.

What If No Cause Is Found?

If, even after intensive investigations by your doctor, no cause for your miscarriage has been found, there are still certain precautions you can take. I would recommend that during your next pregnancy you take it very easy, with as much bed rest as possible in the first 9 to 10 weeks. (In chapter 2, page 32, I explain fully why I firmly believe in the value of bed rest.)

Once you have seen the fetal heartbeat on the sonogram, at 6 to 7 weeks, your anxiety should decrease significantly, which will help give the pregnancy the optimal chance of continuing normally.

Keeping a Positive Attitude

It's important also, when you're newly pregnant again, to try to maintain a positive attitude and not dwell on the possibility of another miscarriage. As I write, I know this can be an almost impossible task to achieve—especially when you live through the dreaded day or week of the previous loss. But since stress and emotional anxiety may play some part in future miscarriages, and especially if you experience a lot of chronic fear, I would recommend consulting your doctor, a therapist, or a social worker to help you deal with those feelings. There can be so much guilt, and maybe the previous miscarriage caused problems between you and your husband. You will need to keep these feelings under a certain amount of control.

Finding Your Way to a Normal Pregnancy

If your doctor is monitoring your pregnancy hormone levels and checking up on the pregnancy (with regular ultrasound scans), and if you make it past the sometimes tricky period between the 9th and 13th week, by which stage the placenta has developed fully, you can slowly resume more normal activities. Your doctor will continue to see you often to ensure that all continues to go well.

How Do You Find the Strength to Go On?

Now I want to give you the story of a remarkably strong and courageous woman, Paula, who finally was able to give birth to a delightful daughter after years of alternating hope and despair, years through which she and her husband endured *eight* miscarriages and during which they reached a point where they felt they just could not carry on.

Paula was diagnosed as having an incompetent cervix and some hormonal problems, but with nearly eight months of bed rest to her credit, she finally managed to give her story a happy ending.

Like so many of the other women who gave their time to

tell their stories for this book, Paula may be an inspiration to those whose faith and hope are beginning to wear thin.

"When We First Married, My Husband and I Assumed We'd Have a Big Family"

My first pregnancy was fourteen years ago. We'd been married a little over a year, I was twenty-four years old then and in my last year at college. I became pregnant in the summer, and the baby was expected early the next year. But I miscarried at 4 ½ months. We were surprised because everything had seemed so normal. I remember that for a week or so I'd had a watery discharge, but of course being young I had not worried. Then I'd begun to get tremendous pains, which were obviously contractions. I lay down, but the frequency of the pains began to tell me I was in labor.

My husband rushed me to the hospital, but by that night I'd lost the baby. The waters had apparently broken. I began to bleed and the baby was dead on coming out. During the pregnancy, my only complaint was of a pain on my right side. By way of explanation the doctor had said that a high percentage of first pregnancies do end in miscarriage and that he would put in a Shirodkar stitch (a stitch placed around the cervix to hold the pregnancy) next time.

You go into pregnancy expecting a full-term baby and then suddenly you're faced with a miscarriage. To get over it, you become encouraged that the next time will be fine. So, within three months, I was pregnant again, actually within the same year. The doctor put in the stitch at 10 weeks. We went to see relatives for Christmas, and by the time we got back it was all over again. The stitch didn't help. This miscarriage was rapid, and happened at the same sort of time, 4 to 4½ months. I got up from bed, the waters broke, and I had pains. I began bleeding and the baby came through, even with the Shirodkar stitch still in place.

I was taken to the same hospital. Again I found the experience very traumatic. They gave me a D & C under local anesthesia. It was terrible, very very painful. Afterward my doctor said to relax and wait a while before becoming pregnant again, and I'd be referred to a specialist meanwhile.

So, by the middle of that year, I started undergoing tests. But they found nothing wrong with me. They did do an hysterogram, which was painful, but it came up with nothing. We decided to try again, but for one whole year I could not conceive. Then I became pregnant again, late in the summer. This one didn't go very far. By the 2nd month I was having pains in the lower part of my stomach. I was put in the hospital for bed rest, and I stayed there, but still I lost the baby after four weeks. I was not even 3 months pregnant. All that time, the doctor wanted to put in a stitch again, but the pregnancy was so unstable—I was bleeding all the time—that the procedure could not be performed.

Once again the miracle worked: after the pain of a miscarriage dies down, you look for hope and light and believe it will be better next time. I became pregnant again the next year. This was my fourth pregnancy. It was going well, but then I lost it again at 4 months. At midnight, my waters broke and I was rushed to the hospital. We had moved, and this was a completely different doctor and hospital.

I was kept on bed rest, but, finally, by the ninth day I was so sick, I developed a high fever and began to have chills. The next day the baby was delivered. They didn't give me a D & C, and I was sent home with antibiotics to take. My condition worsened, my feet were swollen because I was toxic. I had to be rushed back to the hospital, where they treated me with a course of intravenous antibiotics before they could perform a D & C. That was dreadful—to miscarry for the fourth time and to suffer all that too.

By now I was a high-school teacher. A different doctor felt all I needed was hormone treatment and bed rest. So we attempted another pregnancy. But I had another spontaneous miscarriage at around the 16th to 18th week. I was experiencing labor pains, bleeding, and, by the time I reached the hospital, I'd totally lost the pregnancy. I had yet another D & C and was sent for a sonogram. There they saw ovarian cysts, and so a few months later I had surgery to remove the cysts. At the same time, they fixed my retroverted uterus, as they felt that the tilted uterus could be contributing to the miscarriages.

Later that year, we came to New York to visit another specialist. I had another hysterogram, and my husband and I went for genetic studies. Finally we moved to New York, partly because my husband was building a new career as a filmmaker, partly so I could go back to school to study for my master's, but mostly so I could be near different doctors and hospitals. Genetic studies on ourselves showed no abnormalities. I tried a different specialist who

examined me fully, and I seemed to be physically fine. He suggested we try another pregnancy.

This was now seven years that we had been trying, and I
became pregnant again—but once more it only lasted 4 to 4½
months. This time, my body would not readily expel the fetus.
Finally, after three long days, the baby came out. As a result I again
developed an infection and had to stay in the hospital a further ten
days.

Then I was recommended, by a friend, to yet another specialist. This doctor felt my problem was scar tissue in the lining of the
uterus. He used *hysteroscopy,* which is a way to look into the cavity
of the uterus, and then he had to go in with a laser to remove the
scars. He also found a fibroid on the left side of my uterine cavity.

After the sixth pregnancy—which I also lost—I said to myself
it would be the *last.* I couldn't go through it all again.

When I became pregnant for the seventh time, we were uncomfortable with that doctor and wouldn't have wanted to go to
him again. Also nothing had changed. We still didn't know why
it was happening. This pregnancy was not planned and, in the end,
I had a termination. I just was not strong enough to relive all the
hope—and the pain.

The final miscarriage, and my eighth pregnancy, was lost at 2
months. And with that I really said no more. But a young lady I
was working with at the time who was also pregnant felt so badly
for me that she asked her obstetrician whom I should see for these
recurrent miscarriages. And so I was given my final recommendation, which was like the turning point for us. My husband has
always shared all the experiences; he came to all the doctors' visits
with me. I was in no hurry to see someone else, but I did keep this
phone number my friend gave me.

Where there's life there's hope, and although you try to deal
with never ever having children, still a little voice would come
back to me saying, What if, what if next time . . . ? I think that was
it, at the back of my mind I felt, What if I try another doctor who
they say is one of the best to see in New York? I just told myself
I'd go and see him for a normal gynecological visit. I expected to
hear him repeat that there wasn't much hope. But, as my husband
and I sat there and listened to the list of things that could be
investigated, our eyes were wide open. Once again, our spirits
lifted, even though each time we had to tell the tale to a different
doctor, it was very emotional and draining.

We had the blood test to see if my body was rejecting the baby, but that was negative. Then we were sent to an endocrinologist. I have always been a very hairy woman, and indeed the tests showed that my testosterone levels (the male hormone) were way above normal. He diagnosed this as polycystic ovarian disease (PCOD), which he told me is the overproduction of certain male hormones. PCOD can prevent people from getting pregnant and may also cause a miscarriage. So I was put on treatment to bring those hormone levels down. It took a year, but in December he said I could try another pregnancy.

As you can imagine, I was still very scared. However, you tend to give yourself the excuses you need, and the company I was working for (I'd given up teaching and was now working in a business) was going through a lot of changes. I thought that if I were to make the most of their medical benefits, I should try now. Besides, both the obstetrician and endocrinologist were so compassionate, I almost felt I owed it to them to try. So, early the next year I became pregnant.

Once we had the confirmation of pregnancy, the doctor told me to go to bed immediately. It was a *very* traumatic pregnancy for all of us—my husband and all the family. I lay in bed and worried. The doctor tried everything he could think of. I was put on progesterone suppositories to help my hormone levels. He gave me a Shirodkar stitch very early on and put it very high up on my cervix. I was put on antibiotics to stop my stitch from getting infected by vaginal bacteria. The medications alone cost us over $100 a week!

I also went in to visit the doctor once a week. Going through my total bed rest, I used to live for that one day a week. The prenatal care was really special, with the doctor and all his nurses being so concerned. I'm sure that helped too.

We had our first scare at 12 weeks. I began to get labor pains and to bleed. I can't tell you how panicked I was. I kept saying I didn't want to go through it all again. But I went in to see the doctor, and on ultrasound we saw that the fetus was alive. We could also see that the cervix was not opening up. The pregnancy, in fact, was still high in the uterus. And the stitch on the cervix was in tight.

I was given ritodrine to relax the uterus. I'd never had that before in any other pregnancy. We came out of the doctor's office feeling a little more confident. This was the first time I'd ever gone to a doctor, complaining of bleeding and contractions, and been able to go back home with the pregnancy.

Later, the pregnancy began to press down on the stitch, and I was told to stay as flat in bed as possible. I had been in bed since the 7th week of the pregnancy, only getting up for the bathroom and once a week for a doctor's visit. But for the next eight weeks I was flat on my back, not even sitting up. Then, at 30 to 32 weeks, on one of those visits, the doctor excitedly announced, "we've got the baby." All it needed was to grow a little more, but if I went into labor then, it would have been all right.

He'd planned to take out the stitch in early December, a week or so before my due date. But on Thanksgiving weekend, we finally allowed ourselves a baby shower, and I sat up in bed to greet my friends. The last person left at nine thirty that night, and as I got out of bed to take a shower my waters broke.

We went to the hospital and the stitch had to be taken out, which was not easy since it was in so tightly. I didn't have a long labor, hardly feeling any contractions. My daughter was born at 34 weeks, weighing 5 pounds 6 ounces. She was perfectly normal, not too premature at all. She was kept in the regular nursery, and all the pediatrician did was increase her feeding times. She was allowed to come home with us.

My daughter is now two and one-half years old, and I would do it all again for her. But having a second child will be very hard. I don't believe in only children, and I do feel she needs a sibling for her own sake. But to have to go through all that bed rest with a toddler around won't be easy. So I'm not sure. Right now I'm in between wondering whether to return to work, or to try for another pregnancy. We're so very happy to have her—but it's all so strange. When we first married, we both loved children, and my husband and I thought we'd have a big family!

We're still not sure what the specific cause of our recurrent miscarriages was. Does it matter? In many ways, I think it might have been the care and extra-attentive treatment I received that led to the happy outcome.

2

When the Bleeding and Cramping Spell Trouble

Y OU'RE A NORMAL, healthy woman, happily looking forward to having a baby. Just like Paula, whose story appears in the previous chapter, you're unlikely even to have thought about losing the baby—unless a history of miscarriages has already dogged you or a close relative—when suddenly events overtake your dreams. You are thrown into an incomprehensible and strange underground world of tears and heartache.

The most common symptoms of an impending miscarriage are bleeding and cramping. Yet bleeding in pregnancy is also very commonplace and, in those who don't miscarry, may be quite normal. So obviously, some distinction must be made between what is normal and what may mean a possible miscarriage.

Up to 70 percent of pregnant women experience a degree of blood loss during the early weeks of their pregnancy. How can this happen when the blood flow of normal periods has ended? One reason is that until the 20th week of pregnancy, the uterine cavity is not entirely filled by the fetus and placenta, and as at all times in a woman's life, your hormone levels may still be fluctuating to some degree. Just as withdrawal of hormones in the nonpregnant state leads to menstruation, so hormonal fluctuations now can lead to blood staining. The bleeding is not coming from the fetus itself, but from the still unoccupied uterine lining, and it in no way presents a danger to the developing life.

This type of bleeding, or staining, for some reason tends to occur especially at those times when you would normally be expecting a period had you not been pregnant, usually around the 10th to 12th week when the placenta takes over hormonal support of the pregnancy from the corpus luteum in the ovary. Or bleeding may occur when the fertilized embryo implants in the uterus, after its journey down the fallopian tube, which can also release a little spotting at this stage.

If the staining is dark brown it usually indicates there is a very small amount of slow bleeding, which has been stagnant for a while. It is not fresh red blood, which would indicate more vigorous bleeding, and therefore is not a cause for panic. But, if the bleeding does become fresh and heavy, like a period or worse, or if there is cramping or severe backache, then there may be a real problem, and you should get into bed and contact your doctor.

As far as cramping is concerned, bear in mind that the uterus contracts at all times whether you are pregnant or not: during a period, during orgasm, and even at times in the normal course of a day. If you have miscarried before and feel some cramping, you are bound to become agitated. But it is often normal to cramp *without* bleeding during pregnancy.

I have found that women who have miscarried before can become so tense over the sensation of cramping that they may trigger a chain reaction known as spastic colon (or irritable bowel), which is caused by stimulation of the autonomic nervous system. This is the part of the nervous system that controls our internal organs. Through this type of nervous response, the colon, or large intestine, distends and fills with gas. The ensuing cramping is from the bowel, not the uterus, and is felt all over the stomach and not just at the location of the uterus. Your stomach will also be distended with gas. Extremely severe cramping, however, needs immediate investigation, as it may be an indication of an impending miscarriage or even a tubal (ectopic) pregnancy.

Bleeding is by far the most common sign of a threatened or inevitable miscarriage. Before I explain the various terms you are likely to hear from your doctor or the hospital staff for the different types of miscarriage, I want first to explain the best course of action to take should any symptoms occur.

What to Do When You Fear You May Be Miscarrying

I am aware that panic is a commonly experienced emotion when things begin to go wrong, especially if you have miscarried previously. But panic, agitation, and aggravated distress, unfortunately, will only worsen the situation, so apart from saying, "remain calm," this is my best advice: First, get to bed. If the cramps feel like real pain, lie on your side. If the pain is such that you feel the need to use pain-killers, then that would be a sign to contact your doctor.

If there is blood loss, you don't necessarily have to call your doctor immediately, for example, if it is in the middle of the night, unless the bleeding becomes a moderate flow (more than staining). It may not be a bad sign.

Anyone might quite naturally be terrified that a miscarriage will lead to severe *hemorrhage* (which is, in fact, a synonym for heavy bleeding), ultimately even needing a blood transfusion. But be reassured; despite alarming stories that you may have heard over the years, although the severity of the blood loss can be frightening, it can be controlled by your doctor.

If the pregnancy is in its very early stages, that is, in the first 6 weeks, there is little chance of your bleeding so heavily that it becomes dangerous. You may have cramps and find that you pass a few clots. It may also be possible, if the pregnancy is still under 6 weeks, to avoid a dilatation and curettage (D & C) if you miscarry. This is wise to bear in mind, because repeated D & C's may increase your risk of developing either adhesions inside the uterus or an incompetent cervix, as Paula so vividly described. But you must rely on your doctor's advice. (For more on avoiding a D & C and protecting your cervix see chapter 4, p. 111).

If you are more than 7 weeks pregnant, then there may be heavy bleeding that can last for several hours. *You should contact your doctor,* and, while bleeding, do not use tampons, only sanitary napkins. Make a note of how many you have used and how soaked they were, even collect all your pads and take them to show the doctor. It may not be possible to tell with accuracy from the amount of your bleeding whether you have lost the baby or not. But, as a general rule, any bleeding that is heavier than a normal period is not a good sign.

Should You Have an Internal Examination if You Are Bleeding in Early Pregnancy?

Your doctor will probably want to perform a vaginal examination to check on the state of your cervix. He will need to know if your cervix is shortening or opening or if fetal tissue is already being expelled into the cervix or vagina. These are signs of "inevitable" miscarriage, one that *will* occur, and there is usually no way to save the pregnancy and prevent the fetus from being expelled.

But if your cervix remains closed, as we read in Paula's story, then you may not have lost the baby. An ultrasound scan can help to show both you and your doctor the exact status of the pregnancy. Hopefully, you will even be able to see the fetal heartbeat, which is the best of all circumstances.

If you have miscarried before, you may well worry either

that the internal examination will increase the risk of further bleeding, or that it will cause the "threatened" miscarriage to become an "inevitable" one. You can discuss this with your doctor. But it is unlikely that an internal examination would set off any miscarriage that was not already going to occur; and remember, the internal examination will provide your doctor with valuable information.

I mentioned in the previous chapter the enormous boon that ultrasound has been to the obstetrician, and nowhere is this more evident than in our treatment of a woman who has bled in early pregnancy. By seeing a heartbeat, we can now diagnose whether fetal *life* is still present, even after heavy bleeding, and we can know with certainty whether you still have a good chance of continuing your pregnancy and producing a healthy baby. Before the introduction of ultrasound (in the early 1970s), there was no immediate way of knowing if the baby was still alive, and treatment was difficult to decide upon.

Your doctor may also test to see if your blood hormone levels are adequate, though it may take a day or two to get the results. Hormone values are less predictable than sonography because they may continue to be at normal levels even when the fetus is no longer alive. A regular pregnancy test would be of no value in determining whether the fetus is still alive, because it can read positive up to three weeks after a fetal death or a D & C. Human chorionic gonadotropin (HCG) is the hormone measured in a pregnancy test, and it can take up to twenty-three days to disappear from the blood system after an early pregnancy loss.

What if You Cannot See the Fetal Heartbeat on the Sonogram?

If you are less than 7 to 8 weeks pregnant when you experience bleeding, the ultrasound scan may not be able to show a fetal heartbeat. (The newer *transvaginal* ultrasound probe can, however, show a heartbeat by 4 to 6 weeks.) You will be advised to return for another scan later, that is, beyond 8 weeks, to make sure the baby is still alive. If at the 8 to 9 week point, there is still no sign of a fetal heart, it means the pregnancy has not survived. Should your doctor at any time have doubts about the viability of the pregnancy, it is best to be patient and do nothing at the time, but rather to wait and repeat the scan in a few days time. After all, your dates may be wrong and you may not be as far along in the pregnancy as you believed.

Once you have been able to see for yourself that your baby's heart is beating, your anxieties should be allayed immediately. In itself, this quick reassurance seems to help the pregnancy proceed more smoothly. Ultrasound scans may be repeated as often as necessary, even every one to two weeks if there are any suspicions, so that both doctor and mother can be reassured. Indeed, I would say that if you have experienced any bleeding in early pregnancy, the use of ultrasound either abdominally or transvaginally could be a major component in determining the well-being of your pregnancy. It has made a big difference in managing bleeding in early pregnancy.

Is Ultrasound Safe in Early Pregnancy?

Ultrasound certainly plays a major role in the management of normal pregnancy and is invaluable when complications such as bleeding or cramping occur. Because it is a high-frequency sound wave, out of range of the human ear, and not a form of ionizing radiation such as is used in X rays, it is very safe. On the ends of the transducers—the probes of the ultrasound machine placed either over the abdomen (abdominal probe) or in the vagina (transvaginal probe)—are metal plates or crystals that vibrate in response to an electrical current. Sound waves are sent out, which are then reflected by your tissues according to their differing thickness, or density. A computer in the machine creates an image on the screen, enabling the doctor and the mother to "see" into the uterus and look at the fetus.

Not long ago, ultrasound used to be of great value *only* in pregnancies that had progressed beyond 6 to 8 weeks. Oil was placed on the mother's lower abdomen, after making sure that she had a very full bladder. Then, by moving the probe of the machine over that area, the sound waves passed into the pelvic organs. This required a sometimes uncomfortably full bladder, and the fetal heartbeat could only be detected beyond the 7th to 8th week of pregnancy. Now, however, methods have improved with the introduction of a special transvaginal probe. It is placed into the vagina and lies up against the uterus, tubes, and ovaries. The state of the pregnancy can be examined and the fetal heart can be seen *very* early in the pregnancy—from at least 4 weeks. This, of course, is a recent major breakthrough. Like the abdominal probe, the vaginal probe is safe to use in pregnancy. The clean probe is covered by a sheath like a doctor's examining glove and lubricated before insertion. It causes little or no discomfort at all.

Ultrasound also helps make intrauterine procedures, carried out in pregnancy, much safer: for example, the placement of the needle when we do an amniocentesis or during extraction of blood from the umbilical cord for special tests.

Both abdominal and transvaginal equipment take only minutes to use and give a wealth of information in early pregnancy. No harm has ever been done either to the fetus or to the mother from ultrasound.

If the Pregnancy Is Viable, What Should You Do Next?

Providing the cervix is closed and you have seen the live fetus on the sonogram, your doctor will probably tell you to go home and take as much rest as you can until the bleeding has ceased altogether. Do try not to feel guilty. You should reassure yourself that nothing you have done caused the bleeding: your daily activities are not a factor in causing miscarriages. But adequate rest may be helpful for settling the bleeding. Sedatives are not given as they do not help and may even be harmful to the fetus.

Whether your doctor should begin to treat you with *progesterone* at this stage is still considered controversial by some physicians. Since the DES (diethylstilbestrol) tragedy, of the mid fifties, we have been very reluctant to use hormones during pregnancy. But, as you will read in several of the women's stories in this book, many women have successfully carried a pregnancy to term with the support of natural progesterone in the first trimester. If your doctor knows that prior to becoming pregnant you showed a *luteal phase deficiency* (LPD), also known as a corpus luteum deficiency (CLD), or if a blood test showed a very low level of progesterone, you may be a candidate for treatment with the *natural* hormone progesterone. It will be for your doctor to decide—unless you have strong objections to their use—whether progesterone suppositories or injections will help tide you over either this time of low progesterone levels or the tricky take-over period of the placenta from the corpus luteum (at about the 9th to 11th week). For more on the corpus luteum deficiency and the tragedy of DES see chapter 3, page 68.

What Is So Special About Bed Rest? Some Doctors Say It Is an Old Wives' Tale.

Strangely, for something so utterly natural as relaxing and putting your feet up, there is wild controversy within the medical profession. But I believe in bed rest's value in pregnancy for many reasons. As you read in Paula's story, she had a very bad history of multiple miscarriages. After the eighth one, she remained in bed for most of the eight months of the pregnancy in which the *only live birth* occurred. I was friendly with an eminent European obstetrician. He also believed strongly in the value of bed rest. One of his patients (a well-known film star) was a recurrent miscarrier in whom no cause could be found for the pregnancy losses. He treated her successfully just by keeping her in bed throughout the pregnancy. Of course, her husband built her a special hospital in which to spend her time!

You might well read articles saying there is no scientific evidence to support the theory that bed rest is of value in treating miscarriers or bleeding in pregnancy. The opposing attitude, in fact, is that it does not matter whether you hang curtains, or stay in bed, the outcome of the pregnancy will not be affected. I just happen to believe it does make a difference. And the evidence from my patients, even though it is anecdotal, seems to support this view.

Certainly, the value of bed rest in these high-risk pregnancies is difficult to prove scientifically. To do so, many women would have to agree to be part of a research study, whereby they would retire to their beds for the whole of their pregnancies in special metabolic rooms. There, we could measure stress hormones and conduct other tests on the fetus, to show whether bed rest helps in the pregnancy or not. Some in the study would have to be women who have never miscarried, and others would need to be recurrent miscarriers. Obviously this would be impossible both practically and ethically.

We suspect, however, that something very traumatic—such as loss of a job, being assaulted, or the death of a close relative—could trigger a miscarriage. Such a shock would increase the levels of stress hormones, which may be a factor leading to the miscarriage.

But my major argument in support of bed rest is that Nature planned it this way. It's our modern sophisticated minds that have tried to override Nature's dictates. In the first trimester, the hormonal balance of normal early pregnancy makes a woman very sleepy, fatigued, unable often to deal with the pressures of her work. Most women give up their exercise regimes at this time, because they are feeling nauseated and overly tired. Many lose their sexual desire (libido). All these energy levels usually return during a healthy pregnancy after the 10th to 12th week (midtrimester), when the placenta has safely moved into action.

I think it is best to mimic Nature—she's smarter than any doctor. Why, we should ask ourselves, does Nature make things happen this way? Although nothing has been proven to support my theory, it is likely that the tiny corpus luteum in the ovary, valiantly supporting the pregnancy in the first trimester, needs all the help it can muster. The corpus luteum has a very high metabolic rate, with equally high requirements for blood and oxygen.

It is more than likely that our modern lifestyle has taken us away from what was meant to be a naturally sleepy and lazy time. Newly pregnant women may find they suffer chronic tiredness, whether they are rushing to work through Grand Central Station or looking after a toddler at home. Whatever you can do to reduce your stress levels, at this all important time in the pregnancy, will be of great help. You want to give your baby the best possible chance in the beginning.

Remember, I am talking about patients who miscarry. Not every woman has to stay in bed the whole time, please don't misunderstand me. I'm also not talking about twenty-four hours in your pajamas, for the average pregnancy. What I am talking about is lying around, reading a magazine or a book, watching TV, talking on the phone, just reclining. If there are any signs of a threatened miscarriage, *don't go in to work.*

Not only will you feel better for relaxing, but I've no doubt in my mind that it helps the pregnancy. So, if you have previously miscarried or are fearful, then I would take the action yourself when next you become pregnant. *Discuss it with your doctor.* You don't have to give up work altogether, just try and organize a less-pressured schedule. Make sure you sit with your feet up for several hours a day; either while still at work, by taking off early, or by arranging to do some of your work at home.

In fact, I have often wondered why in completely normal,

uncomplicated pregnancies women, with the consent of their employers and insurance companies, take off the last weeks of their pregnancies. It would seem more sensible and more beneficial to take off the *early* weeks, when they are feeling tired, irritable, nauseated, and possibly unable to cope with the demands of work.

My last point in favor of bed rest is that it certainly can do *no harm.* In itself, it is not expensive, though of course giving up work for several weeks or months may prove to be expensive for you and your husband. Or, if you already have a toddler at home, and this is a second pregnancy, bed rest may mean hiring someone to help at home. So, yes, there are definitely related expenses. But, I know from working with women who have suffered miscarriages that most would do anything to help produce a healthy, full-term baby.

What About Intercourse?

I'm sure it is hardly necessary to point out that intercourse is inadvisable in early pregnancy if you are experiencing cramping or bleeding or have a history of recurrent miscarriages. As I mentioned before, having had intercourse the night before spotting began is *not* likely to be the cause of the threatened miscarriage. But, it is known that *prostaglandins* in semen can stimulate uterine muscle activity and therefore increase contractions. If you have noticed any danger signals, you'd be better off abstaining until your doctor feels the pregnancy is secure. Do discuss it with him, however, if you and your husband desire intercourse, as this may still be the best way to alleviate your anxieties and feel you are communicating well as a couple. My advice would then be to avoid deep penetration and to use condoms so the semen does not enter the vagina, thus avoiding the possible effects of prostaglandins mentioned earlier.

One other reason for abstaining is that bacteria can be

carried on the sperm. If your cervix is short, or open (that is, if you have a weak, or incompetent, cervix), the sperm may enter into the uterus through the cervix, possibly infecting the membranes and then the fetus. As you will read in chapter 6 (page 152), we do know that chlamydia, one of the most common of the sexually transmitted diseases, is a cause of miscarriages.

The danger of contracting chlamydia, as well as AIDS, is a good enough reason for using condoms if you are sexually active with more than one partner. Chlamydial infections are being diagnosed more and more in young patients. Potentially, chlamydia can damage the fallopian tubes and lead to problems with fertility when you do want to become pregnant.

Patients Who Have Miscarried and Their Doctor

At this point, I want to emphasize that your relationship with your doctor may be significant to the outcome of your pregnancy if you have previously miscarried. I do think you should be looked after by a doctor whom you like and respect, who is available to you, who will answer your phone calls, and who will treat you without belittling your concerns.

A woman who has miscarried more than once may need to be seen more often by her physician, even as much as *once or twice a week* in early pregnancy if need be! The reassurance of knowing your doctor is involved and cares is, in itself, a great reducer of stress. Just to be able to voice your fears, or be seen regularly, will ease your mind.

Reassurance that everything will be all right—because your doctor is accessible—is often the best medicine. For example, someone having an asthma attack may begin to feel better as soon as they are seen by a doctor, even before they are given the medicine to break the attack. We're noticing a similar effect on women who have gone into premature labor. After 28 weeks, if a woman begins early labor contractions, she may find that just reaching the hospital—and being seen by the doctors and nurses—helps the contractions subside, even before being put on medication (which may ultimately not be needed).

What Do the Different Terms Used for a Miscarriage Mean?

Threatened Miscarriage

The terminology relating to miscarriage is surprisingly confusing to most people. For example, the term *spontaneous abortion* is synonymous in medicine with *miscarriage.* I know it is upsetting to hear the term *abortion* in relation to your much-desired pregnancy, and some women have been heartbroken to read on their records—after the tragic early loss of a pregnancy—the diagnosis spontaneous abortion. But, until the medical profession makes a distinction between the two terms, just remember that they are interchangeable. If you are suffering from cramping and bleeding, you are more than likely to be told that you have a "threatened abortion," as opposed to a "threatened miscarriage."

The term *threatened abortion,* or *miscarriage,* refers to a situation in early pregnancy, in which you have lost some blood and may feel some very slight cramping. It is usually painless though. The blood is often bright red or else brown. As I described earlier, this is very common, occurring in 60 to 70 percent of pregnancies, and it usually settles down on its own.

If the pregnancy proceeds, you don't have to worry about the bleeding adversely affecting the baby, since the blood comes from unoccupied areas of the uterus, not from the fetus itself. All studies have shown that bleeding in early pregnancy does not cause any abnormality to the baby; the chances of having a normal healthy baby are the same as though no bleeding had occurred. However, it may cause the baby to weigh slightly less at birth. So, unless the bleeding becomes heavy, don't panic. Do get to bed and call your doctor during normal working hours. If, however, the bleeding increases, then you should call your doctor at any time.

Inevitable Miscarriage

When the bleeding becomes painful and is accompanied by severe cramping, the uterus may already be expelling the fetus. And when your doctor examines you, he or she may find that the cervix is already opening, at which point you may be told that the miscarriage is *inevitable.* Although this can sound harsh and cold to you, it means there really is little hope of saving the pregnancy. You will probably be offered a D & C, rather than having to go home to endure the cramps until the miscarriage occurs naturally. Even so, you still might require an aspiration if some tissue is left behind. If your pregnancy is slightly more advanced, beyond 9 weeks, and you are told that you are going to miscarry, your doctor will probably advise you not to go home, where you would await the natural abortion. Rather, you will be encouraged to have a D & C, either in his office or at the hospital, to avoid an emergency situation from heavy bleeding.

Collecting the Tissue   This is hardly pleasant, but I do wish to emphasize that if you find yourself miscarrying at home, it is advisable to collect blood and tissue when possible. Even though you may not be able to distinguish tissue from clots, the best advice is to collect all that is expelled in a clean sterile container, adding nothing to it. Then take it to your doctor or the hospital. It can be stored in the refrigerator for a few hours if necessary. The sample you take to your doctor will help him decide if you have miscarried or not; he may also want to send it for pathology or genetic studies.

Some miscarriages are caused by genetic, or chromosomal, abnormalities. If this is found to be the cause of your miscarriage, then at least you can be reassured that, first, a cause was found and, second, that it is *unlikely* to recur. Contrary to popular belief, if a chromosomal defect is discovered, particularly in a first pregnancy, it need not happen again. Statistically, after the first miscarriage, about 30 percent of subsequent miscarriages are caused by chromosomal abnormalities.

Fetal tissue (and other products of conception) is tested at a genetics center. The information can be of help to you in future pregnancies. In a slightly more advanced pregnancy, a wholly formed fetus can also be checked for normal structural development, such as of the heart and lungs. The placenta, too, may be sent to a pathologist where it will be tested for infections and normal development. New research work suggests that blood clots blocking placental vessels may cause early (and late) miscarriages. This information is proving most significant in miscarriage research.

Before moving on to describe what doctors mean by the sometimes confusing terms *missed abortion* (or *miscarriage*) and *blighted ovum,* I would like you to read about Ruth, who has undergone a variety of miscarriages, plus problems with infertility—a mixture that can occur, particularly with mothers who delay childbearing. Ruth did manage during one miscarriage to save the fetal tissue. I think her straightforward way of describing this experience will be helpful.

Ruth has had five miscarriages, but now she has three healthy children, all under five years old. She and her husband seem determined to have a large family, for she is now pregnant with her fourth. But her story could have been very different, without proper care and treatment by her doctors.

"I Began to Go a Little Crazy . . . !"

Around ten years ago, when I was twenty-nine, I had my first miscarriage. It seemed quite a normal thing to happen, fairly early in the first trimester, at about 8 to 10 weeks of pregnancy. It wasn't very traumatic because I felt it could happen to anyone. And it was not very long before I was pregnant again. But I lost that one too. They were both the same, happening at about 10 weeks.

My doctor had said he could do nothing until I'd lost three.

So I became pregnant again, and this third one was very traumatic. It happened at 8 weeks, and the important part was that it was the *third* time. I'd begun bleeding over the weekend, and when I went in to see the doctor he examined me and said the tissue was in my vagina, and he removed the tissue with forceps. When I walked out of his office, I was in such an emotional state, I never thought to ask if the tissue could be tested.

I found another doctor whom I consulted three weeks after the miscarriage because I wasn't feeling well. He informed me that I was still pregnant. In fact, I'd been pregnant with twins and there was still one sac inside. He tried to help me, but again I started bleeding at home and eventually miscarried at 12 weeks. There was a lot of blood and the cramping was pretty bad. I lay down most of the time, but in the end I went and sat on the toilet. I knew I had to be careful and collect the fetus. I recognized when it was passing because it felt slippery as it was coming out. The fetus seemed to be in a little bag, separate from the blood. I collected it and put it in a plastic container. But, as you can imagine, I was very upset by the whole experience. Now that I'd actually seen the baby, it was no longer just blood that I was losing, but a child.

At that point I began to go a little crazy. I appeared calm on the surface, but inside I was desperately trying to keep control of my emotions. I took my container in to the doctor, feeling very weak. He sent it for testing, but the results didn't give any clue as to why I had miscarried. I then became pregnant again, and this time the doctor gave me shots of HCG [human chorionic gonadotropin] from the start of the pregnancy. At 16 weeks, I went for an amniocentesis appointment. On the ultrasound examination, which takes place before the amniocentesis, they saw that the baby had been dead for about a week. My pregnancy symptoms had started to go away, so I suppose I'd been suspicious. But I could not understand why it had suddenly died, because this time I had even gone beyond the first three months. It was awful having to face up to it before the sonographer. The doctor seemed vague and his explanation did not help. I sensed he felt bad and didn't know how to deal with the situation. I was given a D & C to empty my uterus. The pathology report on the tissue did not tell why I had lost the pregnancy.

All these miscarriages were with my first husband, and a geneticist found nothing wrong with either of us. So there were still no explanations. I was told to keep on trying. But I didn't want to try anymore. Psychologically, at that point, I couldn't do it again.

But life went on, and I don't know if it had anything to do with all those miscarriages, but my marriage broke up. Then, five years ago, I remarried. Within three months I was pregnant. We both desperately wanted children, and I was referred to a doctor who was particularly interested in miscarriages. I was already on progesterone from my former doctor, though my progesterone levels on the blood tests were not low. But I was left on progesterone as a precaution. This time, I went through to 26 weeks, when premature labor started. I was rushed to the hospital, given an intravenous infusion, and put on ritodrine, a drug used to relax the uterus and control the contractions. It worked well, and, once the contractions settled down, I was discharged home where I was kept on oral ritodrine tablets.

At 33 weeks, I went into labor spontaneously. My daughter was born healthy and fine at 4 pounds 2 ounces. Now, at least, I knew I could have a baby. I really wanted to keep on trying for a larger family. So, five months later, I became pregnant again. We just decided we'd better get a move on, as I was then thirty-four. My husband has a good career, and luckily I don't need to work. My son went to 36 weeks, and he was born healthy and fine. Both of my babies, however, have had to stay in the neonatal care unit for about three weeks because of slight breathing problems.

My third baby, for whose pregnancy I was also given progesterone and ritodrine, was born at 33 weeks. We still wanted more children, and I became pregnant again. But this time, at 6 weeks, I suddenly didn't feel pregnant again. On the sonogram, we saw an empty pregnancy sac, a *blighted ovum.* I wasn't really very upset, as I had my three children. But then I had a second blighted ovum, in the next pregnancy, which is unusual because I was told it doesn't tend to happen a second time.

So by then I was thirty-eight and worried I couldn't get pregnant anymore, as I had been trying for three years. I had to turn to an infertility specialist and was put on a low dosage of a fertility tablet called Clomid. Before we were married, my husband had been tested, and his sperm motility was found to be very low. He was put on steroids and a high dosage of vitamin C. And as that had seemed to work before, the doctor suggested that we try the same method again. It was successful, and now I'm six months pregnant again. I've been on ritodrine since 21 weeks and was on progesterone vaginal suppositories for the first three months. Again my uterus is contracting early.

Every time I go into a pregnancy, it's nerve-racking for the first three months, because we still don't know for certain what has caused the miscarriages. The anxiety—and confusion over what is really happening—eats away at you. I hope my attempt at giving a medical account of my pregnancies hasn't been too confusing!

Missed Abortion and Blighted Ovum

Ruth's experience, which fortunately ended happily, included two other types of miscarriages known in medical terms as a *missed abortion* and a *blighted ovum*.

A missed abortion—you will seldom hear it referred to as a missed miscarriage, maybe simply because of the clumsy alliteration—refers to a fetus that has miscarried, or died, but that has *not* been expelled (see Figure 1). The fetal and placental tissue is still inside you. If this does happen, it is advisable to have a D & C—despite the trauma of having to make such a decision—either at your doctor's office or the hospital, without too much delay. First, if necessary, the fetal material can be taken straight to the hospital, or directed to the correct lab, for

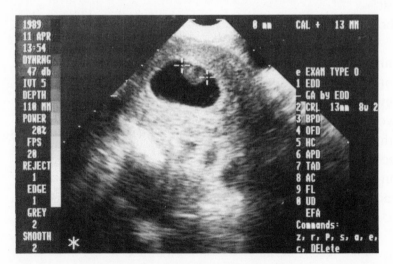

Figure 1. This is an ultrasound photograph of a missed abortion. The fetus shown between the two crosses did not have a heartbeat. A normal fetus would show more body contours.

chromosomal testing and pathology. The fresher the tissue, the more likely you are to receive usable results; it can be difficult for the laboratory to grow the chromosomes if the tissue has been dead too long.

Second, you will not have to suffer the potentially traumatic experience of knowing you have a dead baby inside of you. Third, you will avoid a remote risk of infection getting into the uterus and harming you. Fourth, you will also avoid the risk of the fetus aborting itself during the night, with the consequent emergency rush to the hospital. Lastly, there is the very remote risk of your developing a clotting disorder if a dead fetus is retained beyond about six weeks. This is especially so with a more advanced fetal death, rather than in a very early pregnancy.

What Is a Blighted Ovum? Many women are confused when told that they have a blighted ovum, which means there is not a fetus inside the pregnancy sac. With a blighted ovum you have been pregnant. The fact that your pregnancy hormonal levels (HCG) increased gave you a positive pregnancy test. No doubt, you became as excited as any woman would be about the idea of having a baby.

When you have an ultrasound scan, however, you will see only an empty sac because with a blighted ovum the fetus does not develop (see Figure 2). Normally, an egg, once fertilized, develops. Imagine then, the mass of developing cells going in two different directions, one to form the pregnancy sac and the other to form the embryo. In the case of a blighted ovum, the second stage just does not happen: the pregnancy sac develops, but the embryo does not. You can liken it to growing beans and waiting for the sprouts to shoot through. Some just do not take. Roots may develop but there are no stems.

Weeks may go by without your bleeding or starting to lose the pregnancy. After a while you may have a very dark brown discharge, and your breasts may stop feeling so swollen or sensitive. You probably won't miscarry spontaneously for a

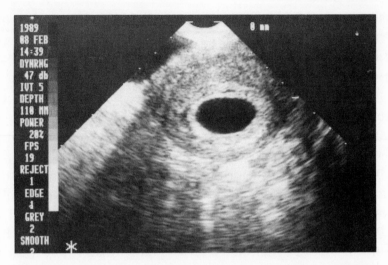

Figure 2.   This ultrasound photograph taken at eight weeks of pregnancy shows a blighted ovum. The pregnancy sac is empty, filled only with fluid (dark area in center).

long time. The blighted ovum may not be discovered until you visit your doctor and have an ultrasound scan to look for the fetal heartbeat.

We are diagnosing more blighted ova today. They are thought to be caused by a lack of chromosomes either from a poor sperm or a poor egg. And it affects older couples more often. One of the reasons why we're seeing it so often is that we use ultrasound more often in early pregnancy and can therefore detect the empty sac. Also, as the age of parents becomes gradually older, there is an increased risk of a miscarriage from poor egg or sperm quality.

Fifteen years or so ago, any woman who went to her doctor because the pregnancy was not developing, or because she was bleeding, was often unable to be given a definite diagnosis. Now, fortunately, we can tell more accurately what has happened by using sonography. But still we can do nothing to save a blighted ovum. With no embryo present, there is obviously nothing that can be done.

With ultrasound, we are becoming more aware of various eventualities: For example, your doctor might be able to see three or four empty sacs inside the uterus. Some women may be conceiving blighted multiple ova. Women have hundreds of thousands of eggs, and men have millions of sperm, and it seems that more often than we realized, more than one egg is fertilized at the same time.

We are aware now of a "vanishing twin." A twin pregnancy is diagnosed, then after some vaginal bleeding a repeat sonogram shows that one of the twins has disappeared (or miscarried) while the other continues to grow normally.

Just within the last year, ultrasound, as we mentioned earlier, has become more sophisticated. The transvaginal probe has been developed, which when inserted into the vagina right up against the uterus, can detect very early pregnancies in some detail. This means we can diagnose a normal continuing pregnancy much earlier than was previously possible, and thus eliminate the diagnosis of a blighted ovum early on.

Preparing Yourself Mentally to Cope with a Missed Abortion or Blighted Ovum   If the information from an ultrasound scan confirms that the pregnancy will not continue—either because the fetus is already dead (missed abortion) or there is an empty sac in the uterus (blighted ovum)—the doctor may initially seem concerned mainly about your health and physical condition and will probably spend less time (of necessity) on your sadness and grieving. This is not an easy time emotionally, even under the best conditions, but you must realize that medical management has to be the first priority. It pays to listen and have confidence in your doctor.

In all likelihood, the doctor will recommend performing a D & C in his office, or in the hospital, and will explain how the uterus has to be emptied. The other method of management, as I mentioned earlier in the chapter, would be to let the fetus dispel itself from your uterus spontaneously. However, it cannot be pleasant for any woman to know she is carrying a dead fetus. Further, bear in mind that holding on to a nonviable pregnancy will only delay the return of your menstrual cycle and the next opportunity for you to attempt another pregnancy.

Other Reasons for Bleeding in Early Pregnancy, or Signs That Are Incompatible with Normal Pregnancy

Molar Pregnancy (Hydatidiform Mole)

This is a very rare condition that starts off like a normal pregnancy. But then, at about 10 weeks or so, irregular vaginal bleeding occurs, which may even be heavy and cause anemia. Profuse vomiting and severe nausea are also common symptoms. When the doctor examines you, the uterus, as well as the ovaries, may seem overly large.

Another indication of molar pregnancy is the high level of HCG (pregnancy hormone), and sonography fortunately can confirm the diagnosis. The condition may be caused by chromosomal abnormalities of the egg or sperm. It is a benign tumor that is more common in women near the age of 40. Occasionally, little pieces of tissue resembling grapes may be passed vaginally.

Bleeding may be your first sign, but it may not start until quite late, even beyond the 16th week of pregnancy. It is usually very dark and has been described as prune colored. The condition may have been discovered prior to that if you had had an ultrasound scan, which would show a typical appearance in the uterus.

The placental tissue grows inordinately fast, producing a mass of cysts, like a bunch of grapes. The rapid growth of the placenta will raise your hormone levels beyond what is normal, leading to excessive vomiting and, maybe, high blood pressure. Fortunately, this is a rare condition, showing up only once in fifteen hundred pregnancies in the USA and Europe.

Although the mole would eventually miscarry spontaneously, a D & C is recommended to ensure that all the tissue from the molar pregnancy is removed from the uterus. Even less likely is the chance that this condition can become cancerous. The *choriocarcinoma,* as it is then called, affects only about 10 percent of molar pregnancies and is completely curable.

Because of the risks involved, if you have been diagnosed as having a hydatidiform mole, your doctor will continue to follow your condition—mainly by blood tests—for up to a year after the D & C. Women are usually advised to wait from one to two years, following a molar pregnancy, before trying to conceive again. About a year is considered a safe time lag if the blood test results continue to prove normal.

A diagnosis of molar pregnancy can be very scary. Not only do you have to undergo a strange, and hardly talked about, form of miscarriage, but it carries with it the remote risk of cancer. There is also the slight risk of a molar pregnancy recurring, so the next time around your doctor will monitor your pregnancy very carefully in the early weeks. Remember though that this is a rare condition.

Ectopic Pregnancy

Although an ectopic pregnancy is not a miscarriage, often the early symptoms are similar. You should be aware of the difference, as an ectopic pregnancy can seriously damage the fallopian tube, may affect your future fertility, and could ultimately rupture the tube, endangering your life through acute blood loss.

No one is quite sure why ectopic pregnancies happen. But the fertilized ovum may have taken too long to travel down the fallopian tube and, on the 7th day, instead of reaching the uterus where it should implant, it embeds itself in the tube where the beginnings of a pregnancy are acted out.

Pregnancy hormones are produced at sufficient levels to make you miss a period and produce a positive pregnancy test. You may not find out about the condition until your first visit to the doctor. An internal examination will reveal that the uterus has not expanded as in a normal pregnancy. An ultrasound scan will not always show the pregnancy in the tube, but it will show the uterus to be empty.

Symptoms to watch out for are the lack of pregnancy symptoms or less nausea or vomiting than in normal pregnancy, some low abdominal cramping, and slight spotting or staining of blood. Other indicators are a feeling of dizziness and shoulder-tip pain. If such pain or bleeding persists, you must report to your doctor or the hospital, as you don't want to delay the diagnosis. But remember, too, that tubal pregnancy is fairly rare, and the diagnosis will probably be of a normal pregnancy, and your worries will have been for nothing.

With early treatment, an ectopic pregnancy can be removed and the tube saved, thus also perhaps saving your fertility. So, if you have noticed a missed period, associated with low cramplike abdominal pain and scant or dark spotting, do see your doctor as quickly as possible—particularly if you have a history of high-risk factors, such as the past or present use of an intrauterine device or infection in your tubes (salpingitis), which may promote tubal pregnancies.

Your doctor will diagnose your tubal (ectopic) pregnancy by monitoring hormone levels in your blood and by using abdominal or transvaginal sonography. When removing the ectopic pregnancy, your doctor will use either an instrument called a laparoscope, which does not require opening your abdomen, or abdominal surgery which does require a wide incision which opens your abdomen.

Laporoscopy is an operative procedure which requires hospitalization and is done under general anesthesia. It requires that you are admitted on the morning of the procedure, not having eaten or drunk from midnight of that day.

In the operating room, an intravenous infusion is started and the anesthesiologist then gives you a general anesthetic. Once you are asleep the gynecologist distends your abdomen with carbon dioxide gas which allows him to pass a viewing instrument (laporoscope) through a tiny incision in your umbilicus. Additional probes are placed through small puncture wounds (at the pubic hair line) to help the doctor to move your organs for better inspection and to assist in removing the pregnancy from the tube.

The operation takes about forty-five minutes to one hour.

You can usually leave the hospital after a few further hours in the recovery room. Occasionally you may have to remain in the hospital overnight. The stitches do not require removal, and the scar is in the umbilicus. This procedure for treating an ectopic pregnancy through a laparoscope is new and is not applicable in all cases. Your doctor will decide on which approach to use.

Complete Abortion

If your doctor informs you that there has been a "complete abortion," this means the miscarriage has brought out all fetal tissue and the uterus is empty. There will be no need for a D & C. If you are bleeding, you may be given ergometrine tablets by mouth to help the uterus contract and so reduce the amount of blood loss.

"Emptying" the Uterus

How the uterus is "emptied" depends on the stage of the pregnancy. Often the cervix dilates from the passage of fetal tissue, and a curettage (D & C) can be performed in your doctor's office using a local anesthetic in the cervix; some Demerol may be given intravenously, too, as a painkiller.

In a hospital procedure, the uterus may be suctioned or curetted, and a general anesthetic might be required if your pregnancy was advanced. Otherwise, only heavy intravenous sedation may be used. Antibiotics are not usually given unless you have a fever or there is suspicion of an infection.

Sometimes the tissue is sent by your doctor to the genetics lab for chromosome analysis, especially if you have previously miscarried. The D & C will also give your doctor the chance to investigate the inside of your uterus for any structural abnormalities. A follow-up visit is usually arranged for two weeks following the procedure, so that your doctor can make sure your uterus has gone back to normal size and there is no infection.

If you miscarried beyond about 12 weeks and the fetal tissue is retained, the cervix can be "ripened," usually overnight, with a prostaglandin gel placed at the top of the vagina, thus avoiding forcible dilatation. After this procedure a slight further dilatation will usually be necessary, and the uterus can be curetted or suctioned to empty it, without the risk of damage to the cervix.

Another method for avoiding damage to the cervix is to use laminaria (dried seaweed) sticks, which are inserted into the cervix by the doctor, again the night before you go into the hospital. Its insertion takes only a few minutes and may cause mild cramps, which sometimes continue through the night. The dried seaweed swells and thus gradually opens the cervix, facilitating the D & C the next day as described above. These are great advances in technique, allowing for fewer complications.

Another way to expel the fetal tissue is by inserting suppositories containing prostaglandins into the vagina, every four hours. This causes a minilabor and an eventual miscarriage with expulsion of the pregnancy from the uterus. This must be done in a hospital and may take many hours. Prostaglandins may cause marked gastrointestinal side effects such as nausea or vomiting. The procedure may also need to be followed by a D & C, as tissue is often retained when this method is used. It is, therefore, less popular than the previous two methods described.

The new French antiprogesterone pill may also prove to be a method useful for emptying pregnancy tissue from the uterus.

After your uterus has been emptied, bleeding may last for a few days or up to two weeks. However, it should not be very heavy. To avoid infection, use pads and avoid tampons, and do not have intercourse for two weeks. Any fever of over 100 degrees Fahrenheit should be reported to your doctor. Your period should return within four to six weeks after the D & C.

What Is the Association Between Miscarriage and Parental Age?

The older a woman is, in her late thirties or early forties, the greater the likelihood of having a miscarriage. Not that this seems to prevent a woman today from attempting a pregnancy if she finds herself in her forties and wanting a baby! As you will read in Margaret's story, below, there is plenty of true grit and determination in such women.

But there is no way around the facts. Men and especially women in their late thirties and older

- are more at risk for developing degenerative diseases such as high blood pressure or diabetes.
- usually have more responsibility and potentially higher stress levels from their careers.
- are at greater risk of chromosomal abnormalities in their offspring—hence the recommendation to have the baby's chromosomes tested by amniocentesis, or chorionic villus sampling (if maternal age is 35 or more or the paternal age is 55 or more years).

Margaret is a lively woman who runs her own business. She had suffered through three miscarriages, all of which were blighted ova. At one time she was scared she might never have a baby because she and her husband are both over forty.

"Whether There Ever Was a Fetus, or Not, the Build-up Is the Same."

I wasn't married until I was thirty-eight. Neither my husband nor I had been married before, which must make us most unusual. To make matters even stranger, I'd never been pregnant. Raised a strict Catholic, I was a virgin until I was thirty years old, which must make me sound archaic!

But now here I was happily married, and we wanted to try to

get pregnant almost immediately. But it took three years before I conceived. Maybe we just weren't having sex often enough, since we were a two-career couple getting on somewhat in years. However, ultimately I did get pregnant and we were both thrilled.

The pregnancy began in May, and I miscarried at 12 weeks on my mother's birthday. I'll never forget the day, because I'd just told her the good news. I began spotting over the weekend. I was in touch with my doctor, who advised me to go to bed. I lost the baby during the weekend. I tried to collect what was coming out, but that felt like a bizarre thing to be doing. I couldn't imagine what I was going to get. There I was in the bathroom, holding a cup. I did collect some clots.

I'd been warned I was at some risk during pregnancy, as I was over forty years old. But we had not expected this to happen. I went into the doctor's office, and I remember sitting there thinking about everything. It all seemed so strange, like a bad dream. The sonogram showed it was a blighted ovum, just an empty sac. He performed a D & C, with a shot of anti-D [an injection designed to destroy RH positive cells; cells which may cause sensitization in the next pregnancy] afterward, as my blood is Rh negative. This prevents my body from forming antibodies to the baby's blood, which could harm the next pregnancy.

I think my husband was angry, or at least he was trying not to be angry with me, that maybe I hadn't taken enough care of myself. Whether there was ever a fetus or not, the psychological build-up is just the same. I was so sad and had to go through a lot of mourning before I felt ready to try again.

The second miscarriage was the hardest because there was such a sense of loss. I was in my forties and pregnant again. This really felt like our last chance, and we both wanted a child so badly. Losing the pregnancy was losing the dream of the child in our lives. I can verify that it takes about thirty seconds, from the moment you're given the positive result of a pregnancy test to dressing the baby in clothes and going out to the park, in your mind. Anyway, this one was also a blighted ovum, which I lost in the 10th to 11th week. Then, within a short space of time, I had a third miscarriage, another blighted ovum discovered in the 6th to 8th week.

There really is no way of logically convincing yourself it was not a child you lost, because in those weeks of imaginings, as far as you knew, the child inside of you had so many possibilities. The pain still comes from the lost dream. To you, it's a baby that has died.

Miraculously, our next pregnancy—after waiting three months—seemed good. There was some slight spotting again, over which I panicked of course and took myself to bed. Since the progesterone level in my blood was low, I was put on vaginal suppositories and advised to rest as much as possible. I brought all my work back home for the first three months. It was Christmas and I really wanted to go out for dinner. I phoned the doctor to ask if it would be all right. He said very firmly, "No. You stay home." At my age, he felt it was sensible to be as careful as is humanly possible.

Apart from some gas pains and a little cramping, all went well. When I was six months pregnant, everything was so good we even went on vacation. At the end, I went eleven days past my due date when my waters broke. I was induced and our son was born, normal and healthy. He's like a gift from God to us.

Midtrimester Miscarriages: After 12 to 14 Weeks and up to 24 Weeks

The majority of miscarriages happen before the 12th to 14th week of pregnancy, but as we have seen in the stories so far quoted, many women also undergo stressful late miscarriages and even lose a baby they have already felt kicking. These movements are usually felt from 18 to 20 weeks of pregnancy and on.

Often miscarriages that happen at this late stage are caused by an incompetent cervix or by abnormalities in the uterus that reduce its capacity. In your next pregnancy, your doctor will be able to treat an incompetent cervix successfully. (See chapter 4, page 111, for further details on the treatment of an incompetent cervix and the placing of a cervical stitch.)

What Causes Late Miscarriages?

Late miscarriages are usually not due to hormonal insufficiency because, from about the 10th to 11th week of pregnancy, the placenta begins to support the fetus with adequate levels of progesterone and other hormones. An incompetent or weak cervix is an important cause of miscarriages after the 12th to 16th week. The cervix opens and the membranes rupture, either because infection reaches the membranes from the vagina, or because of undue pressure on the cervix, possibly from an abnormally shaped uterus.

Another cause of a late miscarriage may be a multiple pregnancy: two, three, or more fetuses may overdistend the uterus to such an extent that the cervix begins to open, though this would not usually happen until after the 20th week.

Unlike first trimester miscarriages, which begin with cramping and bleeding, these middle trimester losses if due to an incompetent cervix usually begin with the passage of amniotic fluid from ruptured membranes, or with a painless gush of fresh blood. On examination the cervix tends to be dilated. The miscarriage then usually proceeds quickly and somewhat painlessly over a very short period of time—hours rather than days—in contrast to the earlier, prolonged painful miscarriages under 12 weeks.

Providing the membranes have not ruptured and the cervix is under three centimeters dilated when the patient is examined, it may be possible even at this late stage for your doctor to close off the cervix by placing a stitch in it, thus enabling the pregnancy to continue. But if there are contractions or bleeding, your doctor will not even attempt to put in the stitch until these have settled down.

Sometimes in the mid-trimester the baby may die and be retained, or it may be expelled following a period of bleeding and cramping.

The Role of Ritodrine in Middle Trimester Threatened Miscarriage

Ritodrine is a drug that has been approved for usage by women who are more than 20 weeks pregnant, to stop contractions of the uterus. Its main use is in treating premature labor, when contractions begin before the baby is mature enough to live outside the womb.

Ritodrine is safe for the baby. The only side effect on the mother is that it causes her heart to beat very fast. It will not cause permanent damage to the heart, just the discomfort of a racing feeling. But, when fully advised of the side effect, most women find it tolerable. Sometimes this side effect can even disappear if the patient remains on the medication for a long time. When a stitch is placed in the cervix to treat an incompetent cervix, and if undue contractions are noticed, bed rest will be advised, and ritodrine tablets may be prescribed if the pregnancy is over 20 weeks. Because ritodrine has not been approved for use under 20 weeks, an occasional glass of alcohol may be advised to help relax a contracting uterus in these early pregnancies.

While drinking is not recommended in pregnancy because of the risk of fetal alcohol syndrome and possible birth defects, an occasional glass of wine will not harm the fetus and may prove beneficial in helping relax the uterus in a pregnancy before 20 weeks. But take alcohol only on your doctor's advice.

Stillbirth, or Death in Utero

Any very late death of a fetus, either in the uterus, at birth, or shortly thereafter, must be one of the hardest experiences for a parent to deal with. There is no escaping the fact that the closer the baby comes to delivery, and to survival outside the uterus, the more violent and cruel will be the shock.

Today, the causes of stillbirth can largely be avoided through good prenatal care and early induction of labor if the fetus seems to be in trouble. Indeed, there are times when a baby is safer in an incubator, rather than in the uterus. The baby may not be receiving adequate nutrition if, for example, the mother has high blood pressure or uncontrolled diabetes.

Severe bleeding late in the pregnancy can also endanger the baby. Disorders of the placenta that lead to bleeding in late pregnancy are *placenta previa* (where the placenta lies low in the uterus between the cervix and the fetus's head) and *abruption* (separation of the placenta from the uterine wall). An abruption can be very dangerous, potentially leading to the baby's death within a matter of hours. So, *any* blood loss after the 28th week must be reported immediately to your doctor and should be investigated.

No one can yet predict that an abruption is going to occur, but we can now usually diagnose it with ultrasound and either arrange further treatment or, if necessary, carry out immediate delivery by cesarean section. A placenta previa is not as dramatic and usually presents as repeated small hemorrhages of painless bright red bleeding, from about the 30th to the 32d week of pregnancy. With a placenta previa the baby is usually delivered by cesarean section as soon as it is mature. An abruption occurs later in pregnancy than a placenta previa, around the 35th week, producing pain and dark bleeding, and the patient may suffer from high blood pressure.

There are rare cases in which the baby becomes entangled in the umbilical cord: it can twist and tighten two or three times around the baby's neck, with fatal results. Or, if the baby has a long cord, it may swim around and through the cord, causing it to knot, which can also be fatal. These cord accidents are fortunately very rare.

With good prenatal care you and your doctor can reduce these tragedies, which is why pregnant women should have regular prenatal visits. Nevertheless, stillbirths do happen, despite our conscientious approach, for which there are simply no obvious explanations.

Ultrasound may help more and more in predicting such tragedies. For example, it is very valuable in detecting growth retardation—from poor nutrition in the uterus (caused for example by the mother's raised blood pressure or repeated vaginal bleeding)—by evaluating the baby's weight and size. With ultrasound, we can now diagnose the cause of bleeding in late pregnancy, and we can differentiate placenta previa from abruption—each of which requires different management. We can also tell if there is a severe fetal abnormality, which may lead to the baby dying in the uterus, and, in some cases, treatment can even be given to correct and avoid this happening. Fetal abnormalities may be accompanied by increased (polyhydramnios) or decreased (oligohydramnios) amounts of amniotic fluid, which can be seen on ultrasound. Also in late pregnancy ultrasound can be used to count the number of blood vessels in the baby's cord (normally three), alerting us to the possibility of fetal abnormalities.

How You Can Keep an Eye on Your Baby's Well-being in Advanced Pregnancy

Now I would like to describe some fascinating new tests that will give both you and your doctor an accurate idea of just how your baby is doing late in the pregnancy. The first one you can perform at home.

Fetal Movement Chart

A relatively new development in modern obstetrics, this chart is kept by the mother at home (see Figure 3). On it, you will be able to record the number of the baby's movements. It may give you a much better sense of something abnormal beginning to appear, and will increase your knowledge of when to notify the doctor of significant changes.

In early pregnancy, the average number of movements per day is low. But fetal movements can be felt from around the 18th week (this is known as *quickening*). They will increase until, between the 29th and 38th week, they are at their peak. The baby's movements in the third trimester are its best expression of well-being. When it is kicking, writhing, and squirming about, then the baby is healthy and happy. In the last two weeks of pregnancy, the style of movements may change from kicking to writhing, as the baby is becoming large in relation to the amount of amniotic fluid it floats in, thus giving it less room to move.

The average number of daily movements made by the fetus and reported by their mothers varies from 4 to 1400—quite a difference! Most will vary from 32 to 100 movements per day. There is no significance in the actual number you report, only in the changes to the number (that is, if they suddenly decrease dramatically). In fact, on an ultrasound scan, we can see that the baby is making even more movements than the mother feels. Presumably only those movements that hit against the uterine wall are sensed by the mother.

Keeping the chart   Select three convenient times during the day, when for thirty minutes you can chart the number of movements your baby makes. Mark down anything you feel—writhing, kicking, or any movement. You might choose, for example, 8:30 to 9:00 A.M., 5:30 to 6:00 P.M., and 10:00 to 10:30 P.M. Choose regular times when you know you can relax and feel the baby. After breakfast, lunch, and dinner may also be convenient. The process in itself will be reassuring for you, since by concentrating on the baby's movements you will know everything is going well. These records will also help your doctor assess whether the activity level is adequate for the baby's size and age.

You might learn from the chart that your baby has sleep-wake periods and moves around more in the evening than in the day, and that for certain periods, there are no movements at all. We assume these periods are when the baby is sleeping. The rest periods will not be constant. Babies in the uterus are not onto a regular schedule of naps!

There will be no association with the number of movements related to your age or the number of previous children you have had. But, if you smoke heavily, they may decrease.

Daily Fetal Movements Recording

Name _____

Directions:
For 30 minutes, 3 times a day, record **each** time you feel the baby move. Do this from 8 to 8:30 A.M., from 1 to 1:30 P.M., and from 7 to 7:30 P.M. To complete the form, record the date and time periods. Place **one** check in each box for each time the baby moves. Do not record totals.

Date:_____ 1 2 3 4 5 6 7 8 9 10 11 12 13 14 15 16 17 18 19 20 21 22 23 24 25 Total
Time: × 8 = _____
Time: × 8 = _____
Time: × 8 = _____
Daily Total = ☐

Date:_____ 1 2 3 4 5 6 7 8 9 10 11 12 13 14 15 16 17 18 19 20 21 22 23 24 25 Total
Time: × 8 = _____
Time: × 8 = _____
Time: × 8 = _____
Daily Total = ☐

Date:_____ 1 2 3 4 5 6 7 8 9 10 11 12 13 14 15 16 17 18 19 20 21 22 23 24 25 Total
Time: × 8 = _____
Time: × 8 = _____
Time: × 8 = _____
Daily Total = ☐

Date:_____ 1 2 3 4 5 6 7 8 9 10 11 12 13 14 15 16 17 18 19 20 21 22 23 24 25 Total
Time: × 8 = _____
Time: × 8 = _____
Time: × 8 = _____
Daily Total = ☐

Date:_____ 1 2 3 4 5 6 7 8 9 10 11 12 13 14 15 16 17 18 19 20 21 22 23 24 25 Total
Time: × 8 = _____
Time: × 8 = _____
Time: × 8 = _____
Daily Total = ☐

Date:_____ 1 2 3 4 5 6 7 8 9 10 11 12 13 14 15 16 17 18 19 20 21 22 23 24 25 Total
Time: × 8 = _____
Time: × 8 = _____
Time: × 8 = _____
Daily Total = ☐

An actual fetal movement chart that you may use, following the instructions at the foot of the chart, in collaboration with your doctor.

Figure 3. Fetal movement chart.

Various stimuli such as noise, external light, touch, and ultrasound might initiate more fetal movements.

From the seventh month of pregnancy, you must be ready to report to your doctor or to the hospital any change in fetal movements. You must definitely treat the situation as an emergency one if there are only three or four movements, or none at all, over a twelve-hour period. Your doctor will be able to follow up your suspicions by listening to the fetal heartbeat and taking an ultrasound scan. If there have been no movements for some hours, it might mean a problem but fortunately usually does not. Nevertheless, keeping such a chart is a cheap and easy test that may alert your doctor to a potential problem.

Fetal Stress Test

If your baby's well-being is questionable in the third trimester of pregnancy, there are two types of stress tests that can be performed for reassurance. *Nonstress testing* will show that when the baby moves, its heart rate also increases. Before a nonstress test, you should not smoke, take any sedating drugs, or drink alcohol. Have something to eat, preferably sweet, as glucose in your bloodstream will make the baby more responsive.

The test can be performed either in your doctor's office or in the hospital. You will be asked to lie on your side on an examining couch or bed so that you can be linked to a monitor that will pick up the fetal heart rate. A recorder is placed on your abdomen. When you feel the baby move, you press a button that makes a mark on the page.

The doctor is looking for what we call *fetal reactivity,* to ensure that the heart rate accelerates in association with an adequate number of movements. The test requires two or more fetal heart-rate accelerations of at least fifteen beats per minute, which should last thirty seconds (associated with movements) over a twenty-minute period.

The method is known as nonstress testing because it does not involve uterine contractions, and the baby's movements are voluntary. The test can be repeated if necessary every three days.

Contraction stress testing (CST) is a refinement of the non-stress test technique. Here, the doctor will intervene to stimulate uterine activity. The idea is not to induce labor, but rather contractions. You will be closely monitored, and the fetal heart rate and contractions will be recorded. For the CST, you have to go to the hospital and have an intravenous infusion.

Again you will be asked to lie on a bed, with a monitor and recording device attached to your abdomen to trace the fetal heart rate and contractions. Pitocin will be administered through an intravenous line attached to your arm, which will cause contractions of the uterus. The test is performed if your doctor is concerned about the baby's health, and if the non-stress test has produced doubtful or suspicious results.

Once you experience contractions at a rate of three every ten minutes, the doctor will watch to see that there is no drop in the baby's heart rate after each contraction. If there is a drop, then this may indicate an insufficient utero-placental reserve, that is, an inadequate supply of food and oxygen to the baby from the placenta. When the uterus contracts, it cuts off the supply of blood to the placenta and baby for those few seconds. If there is not enough glucose stored in the baby's heart to maintain a healthy heartbeat right through the contraction and afterward, then the baby has not been receiving sufficient nutrition. The pregnancy will then need further monitoring, or the baby may need to be delivered if the pregnancy is far enough along.

The Developing Science of Perinatology

Now, obstetricians are working even closer with pediatricians—and not only after the baby has been delivered but even before the birth. There are certain congenital conditions that can be treated by surgery while the baby is still in the uterus. These cases are often written up in the newspapers, as they seem to be so futuristic and part of a "brave new world."

The obstetrician, for example, may be able to diagnose a condition by removing blood from the umbilical cord and administering medication to the fetus by the same technique, while the baby is still in the uterus. This new relationship between obstetrician and pediatrician has given rise to the concept of *perinatology,* reflecting the fact that obstetric care and care of the newborn infant now overlap so closely.

Indeed, you may also have read or heard about on television the exciting new work from geneticists who are hoping to detect and treat, not just diagnose, in-born genetic problems. This type of "gene treatment" will always be controversial, because the procedure allows parents the opportunity to abort a fetus where correction of the genetic problem is impossible. Only for couples known to be carriers of problem genes, the test determines which embryo is clear of the inbred problem by locating genes for disorders such as cystic fibrosis, muscular dystrophy, and hemophilia.

Despite the fears of the antiabortionists, the scientists' aim is to help those couples afraid to give birth to a child, to be able to have a healthy baby. They are basically preventing future terminations by couples who conceive but then must wait for the results of the amniocentesis and finally have to make a decision whether to terminate a pregnancy at about 20 weeks.

I recently attended a lecture entitled "Manipulation of the Early Mammalian Embryo." I found the scientists' work very exciting, and there is legislation before Congress and in Europe that would control some aspects of this type of research.

Parents carrying the gene for a congenital condition may also have had to watch while a much-loved child slowly died of an inherited disease, or they may have witnessed a relative suffer. They are not prepared to bring a child into this life who is so afflicted. So, although to some the technique may ring of parents shopping for the perfect baby, only parents known to have specific gene disorders may one day be eligible for gene testing and manipulation.

How Do Scientists Spot Which Gene Contains the Disease?

Using the same method as that performed to create "test-tube babies," by now the successful and almost commonplace *in vitro* program, scientists collect eggs from the mother after her ovaries have been stimulated to produce more than usual. On average, six eggs can be successfully fertilized. The scientists then clip off one or two cells on the second day after fertilization, when the beginning of a human life is a total of eight developing and multiplying cells. The size of this conceptus is smaller than the period at the end of this sentence.

By carrying out a cell biopsy, and then using genetic amplification techniques so that the cells multiply three to four million times, scientists can pinpoint certain inherited diseases. Other disorders might even be curable at this early stage, by treating the problem with a healthy gene. The eggs deemed viable will then be replaced into the mother's womb. Under present regulations, this work has to be carried out before the embryo reaches 14 days, at which point the cells that eventually make up the baby organize themselves along a line called "the primitive streak."

No physician or scientist can predict who will be born with a genetic predisposition for diabetes or Alzheimer's disease by examining a single cell. But the technology to do so may also be just around the corner. There are, indeed, many exciting new technological advancements within the reproductive field, especially in early pregnancy. Now that we have a greater understanding of how human life is created—and, more importantly, what goes wrong in that carefully laid-out plan—with subtle intervention we may one day be able to bring about changes to alleviate tragedy and the suffering of the newborn infant.

PART TWO

What Has Gone Wrong?
What Can Be Done?

3

Is It a Question of Hormones?

HORMONES take their name from the Greek word *horman,* meaning "to set in motion." They are the chemical messengers of the body, produced by tissues and organs. Some produce internal adjustments to the different systems of the body; others respond to external events and provoke behavioral reactions. As most women know from their menstrual cycle, our individual hormonal balance contains very deep hidden clues to the functioning of our bodies.

Why some women's hormones are so imbalanced that they cannot sustain a pregnancy, we do not know. A surge in understanding the body's endocrinology occurred in 1973, when it was first learned how to measure actual sex hormone levels. Once the structure of hormones could be determined, it was possible even to offer hormone substitutes that have a similar effect on the body, to its own natural hormones.

In the women's stories so far quoted, you have read of suppositories made of the most important hormone in early pregnancy, progesterone. Later in this chapter, I will go more fully into the mysterious dance of life that is the reproductive cycle.

For now, let us look at the explanation for hormone deficiency that, some believe, affects 10 to 15 percent of the women who miscarry. That is a sizeable number of women.

What Are the Endocrinological Causes of a Miscarriage?

I will begin by explaining the specific nature of what is alternatively called the luteal phase defect (LPD) or corpus luteum defect (CLD). Progesterone is secreted by the corpus luteum, a little yellow cystic structure that appears on the ovary at midcycle after ovulation. Progesterone probably has many functions in addition to its importance in preparing the lining of the uterus to sustain the embryo. Indeed, a lack of progesterone may lead to the embryo's miscarrying.

The corpus luteum in the ovary has to keep up this work of providing enough nutrition for the embryo until the developing placenta can take over. The transition (also known as the luteo-placental shift) might take place any time from the 7th week of pregnancy to the 10th week. In effect, that means it starts to happen at about the 5th week following conception (as pregnancy is always dated medically from the first day of your last period).

The corpus luteum lives only for about 10 weeks after ovulation (and conception). So, to determine a genuine hormonal deficiency, your doctor would usually be looking at a pregnancy that was lost *before* the 10th week.

How can your doctor tell if you are suffering from a corpus luteum deficiency? If you experience pain at the time of ovulation (called the mittelschmerz), that means you are ovulating (producing an egg), and in effect you are also forming the corpus luteum. The pain is usually felt on one or both sides, low down in the abdomen. It lasts a few hours and is cramplike in nature. The pain may be accompanied by a sticky discharge that can even be blood-tinged. This is called an ovulation cascade. One signal of the corpus-luteum defect would be the lack of a rise in temperature during your normal menstrual cycle. Normally, if you ovulate well, your temperature would be raised for at least ten days following ovulation. The progesterone produced by the corpus luteum causes a temperature rise (the thermal shift) that should last 10 to 14 days if your production of that hormone is normal.

Another way to test for adequate corpus luteum function is for your physician to do an *endometrial biopsy.* This may be performed in your doctor's office and is usually a relatively painless procedure. A speculum is placed in your vagina, in the same manner as if a pap smear were to be taken. A local anesthetic agent, such as Novocain, is injected into various points of the cervix in order to block any nerve pathways that might be stimulated by a catheter or a biopsy instrument. The cervix is soft, and in itself this is not a painful injection, much less so than when the dentist makes an injection into your firm gums before filling a cavity. By the way, you may feel reassured to know that there are no after-effects to having an endometrial biopsy. You may experience some slight cramping or staining, which will not last long. But you can continue with normal activities that same day, and your period should occur at the scheduled time.

An instrument is placed onto the cervix to help steady it, while another is pushed gently through the cervix into the uterine cavity. A piece of the lining of the uterus will then be scraped, or suctioned, off by means of a vacuum attached to the end of the instrument. The specimen is collected in a little trap container and will later be sent to a pathologist. There are also other instruments and techniques used to obtain endometrial biopsies.

The procedure is performed late in your menstrual cycle, usually around the 25th to 27th day, once it has been established by a pregnancy test that you are not, in fact, already pregnant. To the pathologist, your specimen will represent a certain day of the menstrual cycle, as each day causes a different appearance in the uterine lining. If there is more than a two-day discrepancy between your stated date in the cycle and the pathologist's assessment, and if there is further a discrepancy in the day your period next occurs, then we can tell whether you have a corpus luteum deficiency or not. Even if you are ovulating and producing progesterone, it may not be a strong enough level of the hormone to support a pregnancy.

Yet another way of testing for CLD is to take blood samples from your arm, at intervals beginning from the time of ovulation (about day 14), to see what the levels of progesterone are like. They should rise above a certain level. If your blood levels are low *and* you have a poor temperature chart—which does not show a rise or a sustained rise—and, further, the endometrial biopsy does not fit with your dates, then there would certainly be good evidence of CLD. I'll come to its treatment later.

Why Doesn't the Corpus Luteum Always Function Properly?

The formation of the corpus luteum is dependent on the secretion of hormones called gonadotropins from the midbrain. Psychological or stress factors that have been shown to affect the midbrain may affect its production. Also, hormones produced by the brain work in tandem with hormones produced by the body's organs. When levels are low in one, that is reflected in the others. It is the ultimate in the chicken-and-egg argument. No one can pinpoint which comes first. But stress or severe emotional problems may affect your basic menstrual cycle, ability to conceive, and ability to carry a baby to term, by interfering with ovulation and corpus luteum function.

Overly high secretion of another hormone called prolactin (the hormone mainly responsible for producing milk after delivery) may also inhibit corpus luteum function. And a prolactin increase has been related to stress. If your test shows raised levels of prolactin, you can be treated fairly easily. But often the cause of poor corpus luteum function is not found.

There are many different ways to treat a corpus luteum deficiency. Essentially the goal is to restore your body's good progesterone levels. We now rely almost exclusively on natural progesterone for this treatment, the same as the hormone made by your body during pregnancy. Many women question whether taking this hormone substitute is safe in pregnancy, and whether it will lead to any birth defects. The issue has been raised because most of the currently available medications that act like progesterone are *not* natural progesterone, and these synthetic hormones, known as progestins, have been blamed for an increase in certain birth defects, particularly for a masculinizing effect on female genital organs if taken in early pregnancy. Even defects of the baby's arms, legs, and heart have been associated with the use of progestins. In fact, it has been shown that synthetic progestins may even make a CLD more extreme by suppressing the corpus luteum's natural activity and so decreasing the body's progesterone!

The progestins, compounds that have been made in the laboratory and that can be taken by mouth, have a similar effect as progesterone. Although the risk of birth defects has not been shown from these compounds, there has been some concern because they are synthetic. The FDA nevertheless does not object to their use in pregnancy. Only *natural* progesterone should be used by patients trying to conceive, or by those trying to prevent a miscarriage. There has been no study showing any risk to your baby from the use of natural progesterone either before or during pregnancy. As usual, however, the caveat applies: no medication should ever be taken in pregnancy unless there is a specific reason and unless the risks are outweighed by the possible benefits. Natural progesterone received a bad name only because it was lumped in the same category as the synthetic progestins.

If it is determined that you have a CLD and you are not yet pregnant, then it is a good idea to begin treatment before you conceive—to give your next pregnancy a healthier start. Treatment can be given in a number of ways, and you should follow your doctor's advice. Right at the beginning of your menstrual cycle, you would take clomiphene, which will ensure ovulation, and then you would take natural hormone progesterone suppositories, which are inserted vaginally in a dose of 25 or 50 milligrams morning and evening, from about day 14 (ovulation day) for at least ten to twelve days. At that point a pregnancy test would be done. If you are not pregnant, the suppositories would be discontinued. But, if conception does take place, then they would usually be continued well into your pregnancy, with the backup of hormone-level tests to ensure that the amount of your hormones remains adequate (the dosage can always be increased). Natural progesterone can also be given by deep intra-muscular injection.

Progesterone suppositories are inconvenient in that they may drip or leak from the vagina during the course of the day. Some women complain that their vagina feels dry, and others of irritation. The latter side effect may be from the base chemical in which the progesterone is mixed. You could ask your pharmacist to make up the suppository in a different base.

How long into your pregnancy you continue the treatment depends on your doctor. Usually progesterone treatment is not necessary after about the 10th week—dating the pregnancy from the first day of your last period—because by then you should have adequate levels of progesterone, and your doctor would have seen the developing placenta on the sonogram.

There is yet another method of treatment in trying to increase the body's natural production of progesterone: shots of HCG (Pregnyl). Some doctors give shots of HCG every few days in the second half of your menstrual cycle. But, since treatment for corpus luteum deficiency is still being researched, you must rely on your doctor's advice for the best method in your case.

How Can You Be Sure Progesterone Won't Cause Birth Defects?

Ever since the very real scare in the 1950s caused by DES (diethylstilbestrol)—a hormone that was widely given in pregnancy to prevent bleeding and miscarriage—drug and hormone usage in pregnancy has been frowned upon, almost creating a therapeutic nihilism.

DES, which was first used in 1948, was finally taken out of circulation in 1971, when its disastrous effects on the female daughters of DES users were identified (see page 178). DES is a synthetically made form of the hormone estrogen. It was brought into use because doctors were frustrated about not being able to treat women's bleeding in early pregnancy and resultant miscarriages. It seemed *so* useful in preventing these problems. No one realized at the time that estrogen was *not* a major hormone in pregnancy and that it worked by altering the blood-clotting factors. It would stop bleeding in men, women, or children. It would even stop a bloody nose. But estrogen itself had little to do with pregnancy, and in fact the prevention of bleeding by this mechanism had no impact on miscarriages.

DES had disastrous effects on both female and male offspring. In females, it caused cancer of the vagina at a young (teenage) age; a disease not usually found in women until their seventies. It also caused fertility problems due to structural abnormalities of the genital tract; mainly deformities of the uterus and the cervix. The cavity of the uterus was either very small or misshapen (a T-shaped uterus). These abnormalities, besides causing infertility, also lead to miscarriages. In the male, the testicles may be poorly developed leading to male sterility.

Progesterone, however, is *the* pregnancy hormone, and natural progesterone can be used in early pregnancy, as described earlier.

Can Hormone Therapy be Enough to Prevent Miscarriage?

If you recall Ruth's and Paula's stories, both women had been put on progesterone, yet their problems were multiple. Ultimately, in their eyes, the progesterone did not seem so significant in the ensuing healthy births. This is very often the case. You may emerge from a successful pregnancy wondering whether the hormonal treatment was necessary. But if you have had previous miscarriages, and if time is of the essence, it is wisest for your physician to treat you with the utmost caution. If hormonal therapy helps support the pregnancy through the tricky passage of the first trimester, then at least you will have come through one of the most treacherous stages safely.

The following story reflects such a case, of the doctor doing everything possible and treating anything that could have been a problem. Martha had been through three miscarriages, including the loss of a baby born alive at 20 weeks but who lived for only an hour. Finally, she suffered through a terrifying pregnancy, from which she now has her lovely one-month-old son. Martha ran the gamut of treatments: progesterone suppositories, bed rest, antibiotics for a urinary tract infection, a cervical stitch, immunization with her husband's white blood cells, and daily ingestion of one baby aspirin and vitamins. She tells her story with compassion and an intensity of feeling shared, I am sure, by so many women.

"It Took Me a Month to Let Myself Wake Up to the Fact—I Had a Son!"

My first miscarriage happened seven years ago, when I was twenty-three years old. My husband and I very much wanted this baby and were so excited by the pregnancy. It never occurred to me anything would go wrong. For the first 2 months, things were going fine. Then, at not quite 3 months, I started to spot. The doctor told me I must come in for a checkup. He did a sonogram, which showed that the fetus was not alive. It was a Friday, and I was to go in on Monday morning for a D & C.

I remember feeling badly that I had a dead baby inside of me for that whole weekend. It just didn't feel clean. Both my husband and I were very upset. We cried together but never really talked about it, until four months later when we obviously felt it was safer to talk. No tests were done at that time.

Six months later I was pregnant again. And once again, after three months, I lost the pregnancy. This time it happened at work. All of a sudden I was bleeding heavily. I phoned the doctor and was told to go home, stay in bed and rest. But once back home, I was bleeding so heavily, I had to go into the bathroom where I very nearly fainted, the clots were so huge. I flushed it all down the toilet, so there was nothing left to test.

My husband and I then went for genetic counseling. I work every day in a facility for the mentally retarded, and I'm all too aware of the responsibility of bringing a mentally impaired person into the world—and just how hard such a child would be to raise. I wanted to know if this might be our problem. But the counselor said we were both genetically normal.

Then I became pregnant for the third time. Again I began spotting early on, but I took to my bed, and things were going along fairly well until the 20th week. We assumed all would be well this time. I remember it was December 30th; during the day I'd felt crampy and gassy, but there was no staining. In the middle of the night, at two o'clock, I began having very bad cramps, which felt like gas pains. I began to suspect I was in labor.

By the time we sensed something was wrong and had set off for the hospital, I was already five centimeters dilated. The baby boy weighed fifteen ounces and was born alive. It was a Catholic hospital and they baptized him for me. An hour later he was dead.

This was all happening within a period of three years, and I was twenty-six years old. By then, I'd begun to react very strongly to friends' babies. I was jealous and resentful. I'd also begun to feel that I never wanted to get pregnant again, and I contemplated adoption.

But my husband was not too supportive of adopting. As he pointed out, no one had ever given us a reason for the miscarriages. "We haven't done all we can," he said. "We haven't been told we are *infertile.*" Still I wanted a baby so very badly. Two years had passed since we lost the baby, so I told myself I'd try one more time. A neighbor gave me the name of a doctor in the city—who was the best specialist, she maintained. I remember thinking, "This is crazy; a doctor is a doctor." But finally I plucked up the courage to call, reasoning that I may as well give it one last try.

My husband and I went to see him together. I remember sitting there before this doctor, wondering what he could know that the others didn't. First, he gave me a complete examination and ran all sorts of tests. I'd also brought my files from the other doctors. Then he said, "Why did you wait so long after the last miscarriage?" I told him I'd been looking into adoption. He used those magic words: "There's no reason why you can't have a perfectly normal child."

He ran numerous hormone tests and thyroid tests. Eventually, after an extensive battery of tests, we went for immune testing. The testing revealed that I was not producing something in my blood to block antibodies that were rejecting the pregnancies. I was immunized with my husband's white blood cells. I have to admit that we were fearful because we might be fooling with nature; the procedure was so new and difficult to understand.

For the first 1½ to 2 months, the next pregnancy went well. There was no spotting. But then it started again, about 8 weeks into the pregnancy. I was losing blood. The doctor did blood tests and immediately noticed a problem with my hormone levels. I started on progesterone suppositories. Each week, I went to a laboratory to have blood tests, checking that the hormone levels remained adequate. From the beginning, I was told to take one baby aspirin a day, to increase the blood supply going to the placenta. And I was put on antibiotics for a urinary infection. So, while pregnant, I was taking progesterone suppositories, erythromycin (the antibiotic), baby aspirin, vitamins, and I received my husband's white blood cells. I was worried the whole way through!

Apart from visits to the doctor and to the laboratory, I was on *complete* bed rest. To make matters worse, I was physically sick, vomiting night and day, and I couldn't eat anything. At the fourth month, the doctor put a stitch in my cervix. But still I woke up one night with cramps and found to my horror that there was blood all over the sheets. I phoned the doctor in a panic, crying that I'd lost the baby. He told me to relax, have a glass of wine, and come to see him in the morning. By this time I was resigned to yet another loss. I'd been so sick, and through so much, it was almost a relief to think the pregnancy was over.

The doctor gave me a sonogram. The heartbeat was there;

even I could see the heartbeat! In truth, I felt a little exhausted that it wasn't all over. This was becoming quite a struggle. But the doctor told me the pregnancy looked very healthy.

Two weeks later, I returned for another sonogram. The doctor had seen an empty sac and he now explained that I had been carrying twins and had lost one of them.

After five months, my sickness and vomiting finally stopped, and I began to feel like a normal pregnant person, except for the constant fear every time I went to the bathroom where I would check myself. I continued having regular ultrasound scans. The doctor took out the cervical stitch a week before my due date, in case I went into labor. In the end, a week overdue, I wasn't having contractions, and he induced me. I went into the hospital at 9:00 A.M., and at 12:58 A.M. I delivered my son. He was perfectly normal.

He's so big already, maybe it was from all those drugs I was taking? I'd love another baby but I'm not sure about putting myself through all that again. I'm thirty years old and I realize how lucky I was to have started young.

It wasn't until I saw the baby coming out of me, I thought, Oh, my God, this is it! At first I kept rather cool and unemotional, then I began to cry. It took about a month until I let myself wake up to the fact we had a son. My husband still can't believe he is a father. Every night we go in and look at our son asleep, in wonderment.

The Magic Dance of Life

Why is it so easy for some women to conceive and give birth to healthy babies, and so hard for others? Why is it that some women are fertile, whereas you and your partner, who so very much want a baby, seem doomed to pain and loss?

These major questions, no doubt, plague you almost every day of your life if you have miscarried more than once. There is not, as you already know, a simple answer. But at this point I think it would be sensible to start with a description of the basic female reproductive anatomy, so that we are all comfortable with the terms and concepts under discussion.

The Organs of Reproduction

Although most women today probably feel they know as much as they'll ever need to about their female sexual or reproductive parts, let me explain how they are classified in medical terminology. The vagina is the passageway to the internal organs; the ovaries offer a storage place for the eggs; the tubes provide a site for fertilization and the passageway for transportation of the fertilized egg or blastocyst; the uterus is the site for implantation of the developing fetus.

Externally, you have the vulva, the area between your upper thighs, which includes the mons pubis, labia majora, labia minora, clitoris, hymen, urethral opening, and various glandular structures.

The mons pubis is a fat-filled cushion, covered by curly pubic hair, which is in a triangular-shaped pattern in the female. The labia majora are two rounded folds of fat, covered in tissue, similar to the scrotum in the male. In young girls, the labia majora lie close together, whereas in women who have had children the labia may gape. Following puberty the labia are covered with hair, which extends onto the inner thighs.

The labia minora, reddish in color, vary greatly in size. After childbirth they can project out. Their thin folds of tissue enfold nerve endings, and their muscles can make them erectile.

The clitoris is the equivalent to the male penis, a small erectile body that rarely exceeds 2 centimeters in length even in a state of erection. The clitoris is extremely sensitive to touch, being one of the principal female erogenous zones.

The urethra is the opening to the bladder. Close by, just under it, is the vaginal opening, which varies in size and shape in different women. A tubular or hollow muscular structure between the bladder and rectum, the vagina is the major female organ of copulation. It can vary considerably in length, though it is usually about 10 centimeters long. In childbirth, however, it will distend markedly. The lower portion of the cervix, which

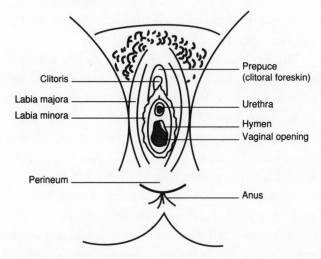

Figure 4. Above is a drawing showing the normal anatomy of the vulva.

is the entrance to the uterus, or womb, projects into the top of the vagina. (See Figure 4.)

The Cervix and Uterus

The portion of the cervix visible from the vagina has an opening in its center known as the external os. Before childbirth it is small and oval, but it changes in shape after your first child. The other end of the cervix, which opens into the lower portion of the uterus, has an opening known as the internal os. The cervix is only a few centimeters in length.

The cervix is composed mainly of smooth muscle, collagen fibers, and blood vessels. During pregnancy the collagen tissue becomes flexible so that it will separate and soften. Normally the percentage of muscle content is low—around 10 percent. However, in a woman with an incompetent cervix, the proportion of muscle in the makeup of the cervix is appreciably greater (the reasons for this are explained fully in chapter 4, page 115). The glands in the canal, or passage, in the cervix secrete a mucus that provides a protective plug during pregnancy and that when discharged at the onset of labor is called "show." The isthmus between the body of the uterus and the cervix stretches during late pregnancy and labor, forming the lower segment or lower part of the uterus through which C-sections are done if needed.

The uterus is a muscular organ, the shape of which has often been likened to an inverted pear. It has a cavity lined with tissue, known as the endometrium, which in turn nourishes the fetus in pregnancy under the influence of progesterone. This endometrium is a thick, pink velvetlike membrane, varying in depth from 0.5 to 5 millimeters, lined with blood vessels. The endometrial cells undergo many changes that, as we saw earlier in this chapter, can be recognized at each stage by the pathologist during the menstrual cycle. (See Figure 5.)

The fallopian tubes come out of the cornua, or angles, at each side at the top of the uterus. They vary in length from 6 to 10 centimeters, and will shrink markedly after the menopause. They also vary in thickness from 2 to 3 millimeters to 5 to 8 millimeters in diameter. Like the endometrium, the tubes are lined with a mucus membrane. This lining is composed

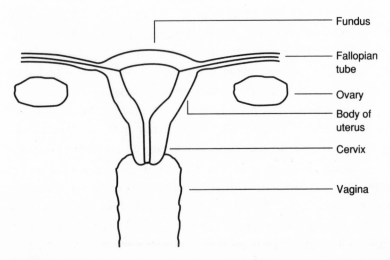

Figure 5.   This drawing shows the relationship of the internal genital organs.

though of only a single layer of cells, and it also undergoes changes throughout the cycle, changes that are important for a woman's fertility. For example, if the lining has been damaged, the tube may not be able to support fertilization satisfactorily and may be a cause of sterility.

Each tube is divided into four parts: the tissue that runs through the wall of the uterus and then up into the tube (the interstitial portion), the part that runs next to the uterine wall (the isthmical portion), and the place close to the ovary where fertilization takes place (ampullary portion). The final part, at the end of the tube, extends in fingerlike structures called fimbria to the surface of the ovary, ready to surround the egg like the tentacles of an octopus, as it is slowly expelled from the surface of the ovary at the time of ovulation. The egg, once released, is transported along the tube by these hairlike cells helped by contractions of the walls of the tube.

The ovaries are almond-shaped organs that develop and produce eggs. They also secrete their own share of hormones. The ovaries vary in size from 2½ to 5 centimeters in length and shrink after menopause. They are located in the upper part of the pelvis, on its back wall, lying between two large blood vessels and behind the fallopian tubes.

The Endometrium (Lining of the Uterine Cavity) and Hormonal Change

There are three main changes to the endometrial cycle each month which are very important in the reproductive chain:

1. Menstrual phase
2. Follicular or proliferative phase
3. Secretory or luteal phase

Following a menstrual period (menstrual phase), the endometrium is thin, since the blood-vessel lining has been completely shed. It gradually builds up and becomes thicker (follicular or proliferative phase), until it reaches the stage when it is thick and nourishing (secretory or luteal phase) again. These changes are brought about by the timed release of hormones during the menstrual cycle.

At the time of menstruation, for example, the midbrain produces gonadotropin-releasing hormones that travel down to the pituitary gland lower in the brain. In turn, gonadotropins are then released; at first, the main hormone is FSH (follicle stimulating hormone). The FSH travels through the bloodstream to the ovary, where it causes an egg (or *follicle*) to ripen. The very act of ripening causes the egg to produce the hormone estrogen, which in turn triggers the endometrial lining to begin developing once again (proliferative phase). (See Figure 6.)

At midcycle, around day 14, another gonadotropin is secreted by the pituitary gland in the brain called LH (luteinizing hormone), and this causes the egg to leave the ovary (ovulation). From the onset of menstruation to ovulation lasts about 14 days, but in reality may vary between 8 to 20 days. The second part of the cycle is more exact: from ovulation it takes exactly 14 days before the onset of your next period, unless you become pregnant. So, you always ovulate 14 days *before* your next period, not necessarily 14 days from the start of your last period.

The moment of release of the egg is not a sudden act, as many women believe. In fact, it takes place quite slowly over a period of two to three minutes. The expulsion of the egg may also be accompanied by a little spillage of fluid from the now empty structure (the follicle). If the fluid spills into the pelvic cavity, it may be accompanied by a little pain or cramping. This is the mittelschmerz—a midcycle sensation of lower abdominal pain—lasting only a few hours. Some mucus or blood may also be released into the vagina (ovulation cascade). Both are not only common, but good signs of ovulation.

The egg is then picked up by a fallopian tube. The pituitary gland continues to secrete the gonadotropin LH, which also causes the follicle that expelled the egg to produce proges-

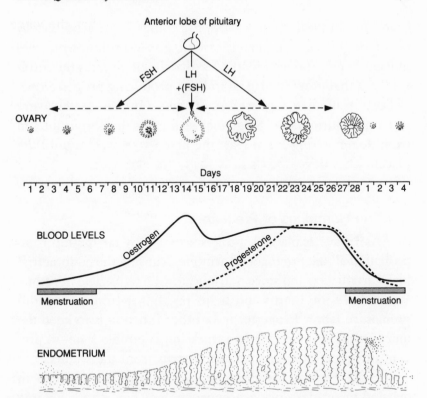

Figure 6. This diagram shows the hormonal control (FSH, LH) of the ovarian and endometrial lining of the uterus.

terone (as well as estrogen). The follicle is now called the corpus luteum. LH is secreted for 14 days, at which time the corpus luteum (which with conception would persist to support the early pregnancy) degenerates and a new cycle starts over with the onset of the menstrual phase.

The production of progesterone during the luteal phase is very important in maintaining a pregnancy. When the egg is fertilized, LH will continue to be secreted, and the corpus luteum will not degenerate but continue to produce progesterone. It is progesterone that makes the endometrium secretory, building up nutrients for the early fertilized egg.

When a pregnancy occurs, the message to the corpus luteum not to die after 14 days, and to the endometrial membrane to continue their secretions, comes from a pregnancy hormone, HCG, or human chorionic gonadotropin, which has in itself been produced by the fertilized egg. So, it is the fertilized egg that gives the signal to keep producing progesterone, to keep itself alive, and well nourished. HCG is another very important hormone of pregnancy as it stops the corpus luteum from degenerating for at least the first 8 to 9 weeks, until the placenta has developed and is ready to take over.

The Hormones of Pregnancy

As I have explained, progesterone is by far the most important of all the pregnancy hormones, causing the endometrial lining to thicken and store nutrients for the fetus. The hormone also sedates the uterus and helps prevent it from going into premature labor. Progesterone's other function is to keep the mucus plug in the cervix in a thick impenetrable state, to prevent infection from entering the uterus from the vagina.

HCG (human chorionic gonadotropin) is produced in massive quantities during pregnancy, which is why it became the basis of the first pregnancy tests. Produced by the cellular lining of the early fertilized egg, it helps keep the corpus luteum alive. Its highest concentration is found at 10 to 12 weeks of pregnancy, and then the level drops throughout the following months, although it remains raised throughout pregnancy. So if you receive a blood test showing your HCG level is dropping toward the end of the first trimester, that is probably quite normal.

Although estrogen is produced in large quantities by the placenta, replacement of estrogen is useless in pregnancy.

Your Uterus, Fallopian Tubes, and Ovaries

If there are any defects with these three major organs, then problems with reproduction can arise. Yet, the incredible part is that they were developed, in *you,* at a very early embryonic stage, so there have been plenty of chances for something to go wrong. For example, the uterus and tubes in a female embryo develop in the 5th week after fertilization, at which point the embryo is only about 10 to 11 millimeters long. The uterus begins as two halves. After these two sections fuse together, the developing uterus begins to create a cavity that is finally completed by the time the fetus is 12 weeks old. The vaginal opening, however, is not complete until the 6th month of pregnancy.

During this early stage of embryonic development, the two halves of the uterus may fail to fuse together properly or fuse only partially, giving rise to anatomical problems.

Similarly problems may arise in utero with the ovaries and the production of eggs. The cells that are going to form eggs appear in the female fetus approximately 3 weeks after conception! At 2 months, the female embryo has about 600,000 eggs. By 5 months, the embryo is storing nearly 7 million eggs. By the time the baby is born, that number will have dropped to 2 million and, by puberty, will have dropped even further to around 400,000.

Women only need a few hundred eggs for the purposes of reproduction, as only one egg tends to be released each cycle, but all women contain a huge store of eggs that slowly declines during their reproductive lives. From that surprisingly large figure of 400,000 at puberty, the number has dwindled down to 35,000 once you pass the age of thirty-five.

As far as is known, women do not form new eggs after birth, unlike the male who constantly manufactures fresh sperm on a daily basis. More than a billion sperm may be ejaculated in one act of intercourse, and they begin forming again almost immediately.

The Menstrual Cycle and Human Ovulation

A regular menstrual cycle throughout your reproductive years has great significance, because each month the drama of life is being reenacted: maturation of an egg (and for the male, formation of sperm), ovulation, potential fertilization, and implantation. The whole system is very complex and is still being researched.

However, we do know about the predictable changes of hormone production, and the cyclic production of eggs at approximately one-month intervals is the rule rather than the exception. It is most unusual for a woman to be permanently anovulatory (unable to produce an egg, and unlikely to menstruate).

So, the major significance of regular periods is that the whole cycle is normal; it probably means you are ovulating and that there is a normal production of the sex hormones. If you are ovulating, we assume your production of GNRH (gonadotropin releasing hormone), FSH (follicle secreting hormone), LH (luteinizing hormone) from the brain, and progesterone and estrogen from the ovary is appropriate.

The ovulatory cycle and the endometrial cycle (changes in the endometrial lining of the uterine cavity) are intimately related, and they are reflected in hormone activity.

One of the great mysteries of the human reproductive cycle is why so few of the many thousands of eggs are ever selected to ripen. And further, why certain eggs are chosen and others are not.

When ovulation takes place, often more than one egg or follicle starts to ripen, but usually only one or two follicles make their way to the surface of the ovary, at which point the ovarian wall becomes thinner. The follicle picks a site where the rupture will occur. The mature human ovum is barely visible to the naked eye. The corpus luteum forms in the ovary at the site of the ruptured follicle. Its name literally means "yellow body" because it is a bright gold color. It measures about 1 to 3 centimeters in diameter. Although so small, it can easily be seen by the naked eye.

The time of ovulation in the menstrual cycle is very important because fertilization must take place within *hours* of ovulation. So, to get a better idea as to when you should try to conceive, start assessing your own cycle by recording the onset of your next period, which will be exactly 14 days after you last ovulated.

As many as 25 percent of women are aware of their ovulation. They may have some symptoms of the mittelschmerz, which I mentioned earlier. Or, they might be aware of a higher basal temperature, which is measured by a special thermometer. Ovulation, in fact, occurs just *before* the shift in your temperature, which is caused by the action of progesterone produced after ovulation. To keep a temperature chart you should get a special thermometer and graphic recording page from the chemist. You must take your temperature orally (or rectally) for three minutes before getting out of bed in the morning. The widely spaced graphic paper will display the temperature shift that occurs after ovulation.

Now there are do-it-yourself ovulation predictor tests to measure the rise in LH, which triggers ovulation, from the brain. Such commercial tests, together with keeping your temperature chart, are among the best methods of judging when ovulation occurs and thus when conception could take place if you have intercourse.

How the Embryo and Fetus Develop Throughout a Pregnancy

The moment of conception is the beginning of the dramatic and exciting development of new human life. The potential fate of this meeting of sperm and egg in the outer part of the fallopian tube may be foretold within the first few hours, or days, following fertilization.

The cells then fuse and immediately start to divide, so that after 4 days there is a mass of cells called the *blastocyst.* This develops little fingerlike structures, known as chorionic villi, which are necessary for the embedding of the developing embryo. After 7 days, the embryo reaches the uterus. The villi start burrowing into the lining of the uterus, and the egg receives a new source of nutrition by opening into the mother's blood vessels.

The First Trimester

The mass of cells begins to form into a fetus and an amniotic sac. As the fetus develops, a cord goes out to the yet-to-be-formed placenta. Amniotic fluid is put into production, and the amniotic and chorionic membranes appear.

Normal pregnancy dating refers to the first day of your last period. But, to be more accurate, I am using a method that refers to the moment of conception (day 14 of that cycle). So, where I say 2 weeks after conception, that would be the same as the 4th week of normal pregnancy dating, or the time of your first missed period.

By the 2nd week after conception, the pregnancy is large enough to be seen by the naked eye. The ovary still contains the tiny corpus luteum, which is supporting the conception.

By the 3rd week, the embryo is 2 millimeters long. Its major organs, such as the spine, nervous system, head, and trunk, are just starting to take shape. By the 4th week, the head is formed, and the chest, abdomen, brain, and spinal cord are complete. Limb buds begin to appear, and, by the end of this week, the heart is formed and circulation begins.

In the 5th week after conception the limbs develop. The baby's own blood cells start circulating throughout its body. The intestines are growing, but they are not yet in their proper place. The embryo is now 1.3 centimeters (about half an inch) long.

By the 6th week the heart starts beating strongly. All the major internal organs, including the lungs, are formed. Growth of the eyes and ears is now taking place. The embryo is 2.2 centimeters (nearly an inch) long. This is the very worst time for the mother to be in contact with German measles (rubella), as the fetal eyes and ears would be directly involved. An ultrasound scan should now be able to show the fetal heart pulsing, and the viability of the pregnancy can be assessed. (See Figure 7.)

By the end of the 7th week, the embryo is about 3 centimeters long (just over 1¼ inches) and weighs 2 grams (less than an eighth of an ounce). Although the baby can now move, you will not feel it for some time yet.

By the 8th week, the umbilical cord is formed, but there is still not a placenta in working order. The embryo will be 4½ centimeters (1¾ inches) long, and will weigh 5 grams (less than a quarter of an ounce).

By the 9th week after conception, the embryo is recognizable as a human being. Its eyes are completely formed and it will now be classified as a fetus. It will be about as long as your little finger, 5½ centimeters (2¼ inches) long, and will weigh 10 grams (one-third of an ounce).

All the major organs are formed within these 9 weeks, which is known as the period of *organogenesis.* From this time on, therefore, the fetus is not subject to major congenital catastrophes, although it may be affected by environmental hazards or premature delivery.

In the 10th week the face is completely formed, and the external genital organs are forming. The baby is 6½ centimeters (2½ inches) long, and weighs 18 grams (nearly two-thirds of an ounce).

By the 11th week from conception, the sex of the baby may possibly be seen on an ultrasound scan (if it is a boy at least). The fetus will be about 7½ centimeters (3 inches) long and will weigh 30 grams (about an ounce).

The 12th week after conception marks the end of the first trimester, when all the organs are formed, but the baby is still immature. The fetus, as we have seen, could not live independently outside of the uterus.

The uterus is now so enlarged that it begins to protrude out of the pelvis, and your doctor should be able to palpate it

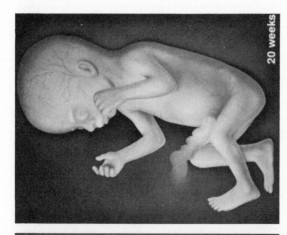

20 weeks

- Fetus almost 10 inches in length
- 8 to 12 ounces in weight
- External sex organs now fully defined
- Well formed eyes, ears, nose and mouth
- Bronchial tube branching becomes evident
- Heart sounds perceptible with stethoscope
- "Cheesy" protective covering on skin
- Hair on head, "down" on body
- Mother may feel baby's movement (quickening)

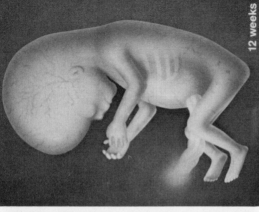

12 weeks

- Fetus almost 3 inches in length
- 1/2 to 1 ounce in weight
- Hands, fingers and nails now distinct
- Feet, toes, and nails now distinct
- Evidence of baby teeth outgrowth
- Most bones have commenced development
- Kidneys begin to secrete urine
- External sex organs become more definite

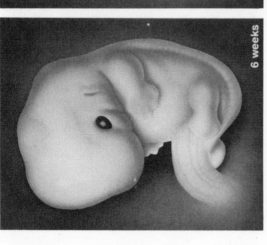

6 weeks

- Embryo almost 1 inch in length
- 1/30 of an ounce in weight
- Inception of eyes, ears, and nose
- Evolution of digestive system
- Backbone appears
- Budding arms, elbows and fingers
- Budding legs, knees and toes
- Formation of face and features

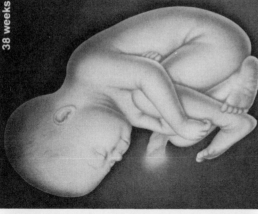

38 weeks

- Fetus almost 19 inches in length
- 6 pounds in weight
- Hair on head now thicker and longer
- "Down" disappearing on body
- Fingernails reach fingertips
- Skin loses wrinkled appearance; now smooth
- Slate-colored eyes usually change color after birth

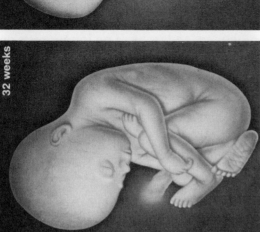

32 weeks

- Fetus almost 16 inches in length
- 4 pounds in weight
- Internal organs more completely developed
- Body filling out
- Eyelids now open
- Bones fully evolved but still soft and flexible

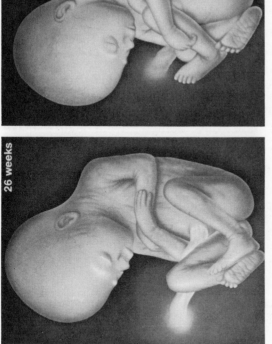

26 weeks

- Fetus almost 14 inches in length
- 1 1/2 pounds in weight
- Skin appears red and wrinkled
- "Cheesy" film covering still on skin
- Eyelashes well defined
- Eyebrows well defined
- Nostrils now open

Figure 7. Stages of development of a human baby.

(feel the uterus with his or her hands) abdominally. The uterus also now contains about 100 milliliters (less than a quarter of a pint) of amniotic fluid.

The object of the pregnancy from this point on is to help the baby further mature so that it can survive outside the womb.

The Second Trimester

By the 13th week, bodily changes become evident in the fetus. The neck has lengthened, and its head no longer rests on its chest. The abdominal wall closes, concealing the intestines, which until then have been on the outside.

In the 14th week the baby's joints start moving; fingernails and toenails are grown. A fine hair called *lanugo* covers the entire body. The baby is also covered with a greasy substance called vernix, which protects its skin from the watery amniotic environment. The fetus is now 16 centimeters (6¼ inches) long and weighs 35 grams (1¼ ounce).

From the 15th to the 18th week, the fetus grows rapidly in both its length and weight. It has hair on its head, and, because of increased muscle development, it will begin to make some very active movements that the mother can feel. There is still a relatively large amount of amniotic fluid in which the baby is swimming. The fetus is now 25½ centimeters (10 inches) long, and its weight begins to jump to around 340 grams (nearly 12 ounces).

By the 22nd week after conception, the baby is about 35½ centimeters (14 inches) long and weighs about 570 grams (1¼ pounds).

By the 26th week, the baby's head is only slightly larger in proportion to its body size, so it takes on the appearance of a more normal baby. It should be about 37 centimeters (14½ inches) long and weigh around 900 grams (nearly 2 pounds).

From the 26th week, the fetus can be regarded as viable— or capable of independent life in the outside world, although highly dependent on neonatal care. Birth from this time on is called premature. Legally the baby must be registered, and if it dies, the baby will require burial. Neonatal care gives an almost 70 percent chance of survival at this stage, but there are many, many risks along the way in the next few weeks.

The Third Trimester

At the beginning of this trimester, the baby is still covered with a greasy vernix, and its lungs are not mature, which of course offers the main problem for the neonatologists.

By the 30th week after conception, the baby is perfectly formed. The head is in proportion to the body, and the baby has a good chance of survival if born. The baby is about 40.5 centimeters (16 inches) long and weighs about 1.6 kilograms (3½ pounds).

At 36 weeks, the baby is considered fully mature. Its organs are not only formed but are working normally. The baby can survive if born now, or if induced or delivered by C-section, and it should not have a problem with its lungs because by now they are mature. The baby is about 46 centimeters (18 inches) long and weighs about 2½ kilograms (5½ pounds).

By the 38th week after conception (the classic 40 weeks of full-term birth), the baby is ready to be born. The fine body hair called lanugo has disappeared, and the baby has early head hair. Its eyes will be blue (all babies are born with blue eyes, though the color often changes within weeks after birth). The nails are properly grown. It will have put on a lot of body fat in the past month to give a chubby, healthy appearance at birth.

At full-term a baby may be as long as 50 centimeters (nearly 20 inches) and will weigh an average of 3.5 kilograms (7½ pounds), though of course all babies vary in length and weight.

Is There a Link Between Infertility and Miscarriage?

Many women who have noticed that they go through periods of infertility wonder if they run a greater than average risk of miscarrying. It might be even more worrysome for a couple who is struggling right now with problems of conception to imagine having to face the tragedy of a miscarriage. But you should not blind yourselves to one very basic fact: the same cause may be triggering both effects.

Increasingly, medical research is coming to view the process of reproduction as a continuum: problems with fertility, miscarriage, and premature delivery are viewed as links in the same fragmented chain.

So, if you have previously been treated for infertility problems, you should be followed very closely by your doctor once a pregnancy is achieved. Your HCG (human chorionic gonadotropin) levels will be monitored, as well as your progesterone levels. You will possibly be treated with progesterone suppositories in the early weeks of pregnancy, as an inadequate corpus luteum may be the root cause.

Bear in mind, however, a point I have raised before. The statistics for rates of miscarriage among such a high-risk group may appear artificially high because of the close scrutiny given these pregnancies. If you miscarry after receiving a very early positive pregnancy test, the loss will be recorded, whereas another woman might not even have known she was pregnant.

The story of Grace and Robert—which I pick up again from their initial comments in chapter 1, where they describe the social and emotional effects of suffering through infertility, miscarriage, and, in their case, in vitro fertilization—should give hope to other couples who may be feeling the odds are too heavily stacked against their ever having their own baby.

Grace said with relief at the end of her interview, "To have that big belly, when you've been through first infertility and then miscarriage, if you can just get beyond your worrying, nothing beats it!"

Grace and Robert chose to receive the added help of in vitro fertilization, when they had already lost two pregnancies from blighted ovas and then failed to conceive again. Although only in their early thirties, which is young for in vitro candidates, they were aware of the pressure of time and pursued their desire for a baby with the utmost determination. In vitro fertilization is no longer considered experimental by the American Fertility Society (AFS) or by the American College of Obstetrics and Gynecology (ACOG). The help that in vitro has brought to the growing army of infertile American couples should never be underestimated.

One in six Americans of childbearing age is now thought to be infertile. That accounts for 10 million men and women. The numbers of infertile couples are growing, too. One in four women thirty-five and over are said to be infertile. But more worrysome, 11 percent of women in their early twenties, a figure that has tripled in the past twenty years, are now having problems conceiving. Couples are thought to have an infertility problem if, in their twenties, they have tried for a pregnancy for a year, or in their thirties, have tried unsuccesfully for six to eight months. With such statistics in mind, you won't be surprised by Grace and Robert's quickly mounting sense of despair at their problems.

"What if I Went Through All That and Then Miscarried Again?"

Ideally, I'd always wanted a baby when I'd be about thirty-two years old. But in my late twenties, many friends were trying to get pregnant and they were having trouble. I said to Robert that we might just find problems ourselves so, a little shy of my thirtieth birthday, we decided to try. After six months, there was no pregnancy. Nothing had happened. It wasn't a haphazard effort either. We were really trying!

So, at that point, we went to see an infertility specialist. He began slowly and efficiently testing one thing at a time. But it all seemed to take such a lot of time. He tried inseminating me with my husband's sperm over a period of five to six months. But that didn't work. It was an interminable wait. I underwent a laparoscopy to make sure my tubes were normal. And on and on, one test after another.

Eventually, I did become pregnant. But I only made it to the 5th week, when I miscarried spontaneously. Looking back, I hardly think of that one as a pregnancy. But now we realized we had to do something more drastic, and we switched doctors. I had further tests. I was given a drug to improve the mucus in my cervix, but I had an allergic reaction to that. Then, two weeks later, I became pregnant, quite spontaneously.

But, sadly, by 9 weeks, on an ultrasound scan, we saw there was an empty sac: it was a blighted ovum. I had a D & C to take away the pregnancy. At that point we weren't focusing so much on miscarriages but on infertility. We'd been so excited at having become pregnant.

The next month I was pregnant again. But it was the same scenario. Literally, the same again. At the 8th to 9th week, we saw an empty sac on the sonogram. That was my second miscarriage.

Now we did recognize we had both an infertility *and* a miscarriage problem, and we found another specialist. This time we were also put through a battery of tests for causes of miscarriages. A hysterogram (X ray of the uterus) showed there was nothing structurally wrong with my uterus. I had thyroid tests, tests for infections from the cervix, and we were sent for bloodwork to test for any antibodies suggesting coagulation problems.

Our blood was sent by Federal Express to a leading immunization center at Jefferson Hospital, in Philadelphia, which is under Dr. Susan Cowchock's direction, to see if other antibodies were rejecting the pregnancies. I knew they only do two immunizations a day, so even if we were eligible we might have had to wait months. And I wanted to get a move on. When we learned that the immunological problem did seem to be ours, we tried to read everything possible on the subject. We were scared at first about the implications. So we checked into it all, read all the statistics and reports, and we decided it seemed medically safe both for me and for a baby. Any risk, even if yet undiscovered, made it worth taking.

We went to Philadelphia and had the immunization in February. They injected the teeniest amount of my husband's white cells (which had been extracted from a blood sample) into a vein in my arm, and the rest of this very small amount was put onto four spots on my skin. Frankly, I was still worried about what it was doing to me. A few weeks later we had to send blood samples down to Philadelphia again, to see if it had worked. Then they wanted us to get pregnant within a year. At that time we felt we were having no problem getting pregnant. But, guess what? Eight months went by and nothing happened.

While I'd been going through the period of infertility, we had put our names down on an in vitro program's list at a clinic in Virginia. I'd forgotten all about taking my name off, and to our surprise we learned that our turn had come. We're both logical thinkers, and we would sit down and discuss everything right through. With no pregnancy happening, we decided to go ahead with the in vitro.

But we asked ourselves, what if we went along for in vitro, which costs a lot of money and carries its own increased risk of a miscarriage, what if we succeeded in getting a fertilized egg from in vitro, but the immunization, which was already nearly nine months old, didn't work? What if we went through all that and then I miscarried again?

We were recommended to be tested again, with the result that we had to be immunized all over. Off we went to Philadelphia, then two weeks later down to Virginia for the in vitro! You lose a lot of time, which is also money, just making these trips. Not to mention the emotional outlay involved.

Fortunately for us the in vitro worked the first time. First, they stimulated me with FSH [follicle stimulating hormone] to help more than one egg release. I produced four eggs and they were able to retrieve three. Then they took sperm from my husband and put it together with the eggs in petri dishes. All three of ours took. Two days later, at a certain stage in cell division, they implanted the fertilized eggs back inside me. It was done without an anesthetic, sort of like having a vaginal examination. Then I had to lie on my stomach for four hours. I was started on progesterone to trigger the brain into thinking natural conception had taken place, because in real life the egg and sperm have not traveled down the tube.

If they can only implant one egg, you have a 17 percent success rate. With two, your chances go up to 20 percent, and with three or more implanted eggs to 30 or more percent.

There are some ludicrous parts to the whole process, and you get to become pretty friendly with the other couples also undergoing the ordeal at the same time. You stay in a motel, go to the beach, and try to enjoy yourselves. But the husbands, for example, have to learn how to inject their wives' behinds with the progesterone. Up to the 5th week this has to be done daily, and then to the 13th week, once a week. It's quite painful for the woman. But you just have to grin and bear it. If you want a baby badly enough to undergo in vitro, you'll take this. At least Robert is a dentist and knows how to give injections.

We returned home, and I was still under the care of the infertility expert. Twice a week, I went to a laboratory to test my hormone levels. But at seven weeks, I discovered staining and of course I panicked. The doctor told me to go to bed immediately and rest for a week. He felt I might have lost one of the three conceptions. He was correct for, at 11 weeks, I went for an ultrasound scan, and we could see that from our three conceptions there were three sacs, but only one viable pregnancy. Following this success, I was transferred to an obstetrician who deals with miscarriages for the rest of my pregnancy.

Although everything seemed fine, emotionally I was a wreck. I could not visit the doctor alone, I was so afraid. But once we had heard the baby's heartbeat at about 12 weeks—with a Fetone—I felt better. I had an amniocentesis, not because of my age but because there were lingering fears that, with all the tests we'd been having done, something may be wrong, and I needed reassurance. At the 18th week, before we'd still told anyone, we heard that the amnio results were normal. We were ecstatic. A day or two later, I started to feel abdominal cramps. I ignored them at first, but then my back started aching too. Soon I was doubled over in agony.

We rushed to the doctor, and he discovered I had a urinary tract infection. I was put on antibiotics for the infection and ritodrine to stop the contractions. From that time on, I was put on half a day rest in bed. I used to stay home and watch TV—I found I was obsessed by "General Hospital"! We didn't encounter any further problems with the pregnancy and I was delivered by a C-section because the baby was a breech, coming bottom first. As I was *so* high risk, and it was a breech and my first pregnancy, the doctor recommended the C-section—which would be safer for the baby. Our son was born weighing 5 pounds, but he was not premature and had no problems. He was healthy, crying, and just gorgeous.

There are still a lot of unknowns for us. Robert is not sure whether it was the immunization that worked, or the combination of treatments that made this pregnancy successful. The in vitro specialists claim that there is the same risk of miscarriage with their procedure as in the general population, that is, it's as safe a method as natural conception. Once the fertilization has taken, then nature takes over. Would we have run a risk of miscarrying that conception without the immunization? Who can tell?

The interesting link between infertility and our earlier miscarriages, which were blighted ovas, is that in those previous cases without the immunization, my antibodies might well have attacked a conception very early on, at the sixteen-cell stage. That would have left the pregnancy continuing in as much as it formed the placenta, but it would have killed off the fetus. It is certainly a thought, that the same cause of miscarriage can make a woman *appear* infertile because she is rejecting the husband's tissue even before knowing she is pregnant.

As I said, we looked into both issues very carefully. The immunization technique supposedly has an 80 percent or more success rate, though they don't have a vast amount of research data yet. I felt, How could we *not* take a chance at this? It just might work.

We were very lucky in that everything was covered by our insurance. Not counting the regular doctors' visits, it all came to $30,000—an expensive little boy he is! But at one point we had looked into adoption. I'd called some lawyers and made the preliminary investigations. A private adoption, including legal fees, would have cost us over $20,000. We would have been putting up close to $15,000 in advance! This way, not only did insurance cover most of the cost, but we have our *own* baby.

But the whole pregnancy, in many ways, was a tremendous emotional burden. I felt depressed and inadequate throughout most of it. I was not like a normal pregnant woman, proudly showing off her belly. I mean you never treat yourself with confidence. At the 16th week of the pregnancy, the doctor said we could have sexual intercourse again. But with all the fears of premature labor, it wasn't worth taking the risk. I'd have been too afraid.

After one miscarriage, they say it can happen to anyone. Then, after two, they say encouragingly, well at least you can get pregnant. But you *know* nothing is working right. With so many women trying to get pregnant later in life, the percentage of people going through what we did must be increasing.

One thing I feel guilty about now is that with all the problems involved, you almost don't focus on the baby. You just think about getting through this stage of your life: the tests, the pressures. And then our son is marvelous. When I'm asked if we'll have a second baby, I say who knows? Could we bear to go through the same process again?

You see, we still can never feel like a normal couple. There are so many scars. All that waiting in doctors' offices, wondering what will happen, and worrying. We would have to be looking at timetables, how to organize, putting the plan back into operation. For example, we'd likely have to wait at least a year for in vitro again, so we should be putting our name down, if a natural pregnancy doesn't occur, within six months. Then, once we've registered there, will we have to be scheduled for immunization again?

I believe we must give ourselves time to enjoy this baby first. We mustn't lose sight of the fact that we have a wonderful baby, to whom we want to give all our attention and energy. It still seems like a miracle to us that we have him—we're so very lucky.

4

Is Something Wrong with the Uterus or Cervix?

PREVIOUSLY I have referred to the fact that an incompetent cervix is a very common cause of second trimester miscarriages (those occuring sometime between the 13th to the 24th week). Now I want to focus on the known reasons why incompetent cervix occurs and what can be done about it.

In chapter 3 (page 77), I discussed the female anatomy and process of development of the embryo, pointing out how very early in the life of the embryo the sexual organs are created. It is now well known that congenital abnormalities (meaning those anomalies you are born with) of the uterus can cause second trimester miscarriages. Some first trimester miscarriages even share this cause. For this reason, one of the major points of investigation for any doctor will be your medical history relating to the uterus.

The fallopian tubes, uterus, and the upper portion of the vagina are all formed within the first 5 to 6 weeks following conception (again I am using a more accurate method of dating; see page 88) from two structures known as the *müllerian* or *wolffian* ducts. The müllerian ducts form the reproductive organs, and the wolffian ducts form the kidneys and urinary tract. Both are of vital importance in the developing female fetus. Between the 6th and 7th weeks following conception, these ducts begin a process of change, during which problems might occur.

In the 9th week, the two müllerian ducts cross above the wolffian tract, where they fuse in the middle of the body to form a single cavity that will become the uterus and vagina. (In the male embryo, the same cavity will have degenerated by the 10th week.) The vagina does not open as a canal, however, until the 20th to the 22nd week. At any stage during this normal course of fusion something can go wrong.

Heredity may play a part in the abnormalities, or drugs such as DES taken by your mother could also be responsible. DES not only damaged the vagina in many female fetuses, but it led to a special form of uterine abnormality known as the *T-shaped* uterus.

The basic differences in uterine shapes are illustrated in Figure 8.

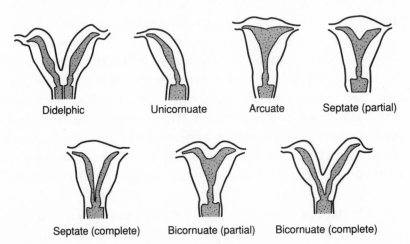

| Didelphic | Unicornuate | Arcuate | Septate (partial) |

| Septate (complete) | Bicornuate (partial) | Bicornuate (complete) |

Figure 8.   Some of the uterine abnormalities which can occur. In the middle of the lower row is one of the more common abnormalities found.

The most common diagnosis, in about 50 percent of cases, is of a *bicornuate,* or a *septate,* uterus, where a band extends down the middle of the uterus toward the cervix. With a *didelphic* uterus, there are two separate cornua, or horns, of the uterus, and two separate cervices too.

Some of the more common abnormalities may have been caused by one or both of the müllerian ducts failing to develop, leading to an absence of one-half of the uterus. Or, the ducts may have failed to fuse, leaving uterine structures without proper cavities.

Such abnormalities of the uterus are more common than doctors used to think. Studies performed on women who are evaluated for infertility show congenital abnormalities of the uterus as frequently as 1 to 10 percent of this population. However, in a recently reported study of women sterilized through the cervix, the incidence was 1.9 percent. This latter figure is probably more typical for the general population, in that this was a group of women not experiencing trouble conceiving. Nevertheless, a statistic of nearly 2 percent is still a very high one.

How Do We Discover These Anomalies?

If your doctor feels that your history indicates structural defects—typically that would include unexplained recurrent miscarriages in the second trimester—the procedure known as hysterogram (HSG) will usually be performed. A radiopaque dye is injected through the cervix to fill the cervical canal, uterus, and tubes.

This X-ray procedure allows the radiologist to see clearly the dye passing as it is injected, giving the shapes of the relevant parts in the cervix, uterine cavity, and tubes. Unfortunately, it can be quite uncomfortable, leading to cramping that may be moderate or, in some cases, severe. You would be advised to request an experienced and sympathetic radiologist. Though it is not usually performed under a general anesthetic, a local anesthetic can be given in the cervix. You may also be given antibiotics, before and after the procedure, to avoid any risk of infection from the dye being injected. You should try and arrange the date of the procedure for just after a period to make sure you are not pregnant during the exposure to X rays.

Certain other terms you may hear in the course of such investigations will include *laparoscopy,* which is the method of inspecting the uterus and tubes by looking through an instrument (laparoscope) inserted through the umbilicus (belly button). Prior to insertion of the laparoscope, your stomach is filled with 3 liters of carbon dioxide gas. The laparoscope is used for direct visual examination to support a diagnosis. You will be brought into the hospital for a day, as the procedure is performed under a general anesthetic.

At laparoscopy, a double uterus or a partially split uterus may be seen. The doctor can also see whether your tubes are bound by adhesions, or whether there is endometriosis in the pelvis. Dye is injected to see if it spills readily through the tubes. Your appendix will also be checked to see whether it is healthy. Following the procedure, you will have a few stitches in the umbilicus and possibly a stitch in your pubic hair region where a probe may have been placed. The stitches will not need to be removed because they dissolve on their own.

Hysteroscopy is a relatively new technique that also provides visual examination, but this time of the inside of your uterus. The entry is made from below, through the vagina and cervix, using a special fiber-optic hysteroscope. For this procedure, the cervix is dilated, using a cervical block or general anesthetic, and the uterus is inspected along all its walls to look for abnormalities such as congenital bands or adhesions. These can be treated at the same time, through the hysteroscope, making it a very helpful test.

Now your doctor can confirm his diagnosis and define any abnormalities. These types of investigations once would only have been performed on women with infertility problems. But now, more and more, they are being used on women with a history of miscarriage. This procedure which corrects uterine deformities from inside the uterus, performed with the help of the hysteroscope, may avoid the need for abdominal surgery to correct the shape of the uterus (known as *metroplasty*). As with any form of abdominal surgery this would mean not only the involvement of general anesthesia and a lengthy recovery time, but also the uterus being opened up, which may lead to problems in a future pregnancy.

Following corrective surgery on the uterus, the success rate for a healthy birth is about 80 percent. But, as ever, the advantages of surgical techniques have to be weighed against possible risks. Surgery may cause scarring of the uterus, which could affect your fertility. Where surgery is not required to correct a congenital abnormality of the uterus, treatment may vary from doing nothing, to placing a suture in the cervix when you next become pregnant. (See page 115 for detailed information on this method of treatment.)

Ultrasound is also now being used as yet another technique to diagnose abnormal uterine structures. Ultrasound carries the advantage of being safe and painless. But it does require an *expert* sonographer to interpret what is being seen on the screen. Until more expertise is gained, ultrasound is mainly used as a screening procedure prior to something like a hysterogram.

A simple test often done in the doctor's office to see if your cervix is incompetent (weak) and in need of a stitch is to pass metal dilators (Hegar size 6) gently into your cervix. If they pass easily, that will mean you have an incompetent cervix.

Other Forms of Uterine Abnormalities Which May Cause Miscarriages

The visual examination techniques—hysteroscopy and hysterography (X rays), and ultrasound—may also reveal that you have *uterine adhesions* in the cavity, known medically as Asherman syndrome if they are multiple. It can be hard to describe the adhesions to patients who find it difficult to visualize such a problem. Basically, they are pieces of scar tissue, or bands, that crisscross the lining of the womb (endometrium) like a spider's web from one side wall to another. They have long been identified as a cause of infertility. Indeed, they are found in 68 percent of women with infertility problems who have had two or more D & C's. We now know they may play a role as regards miscarriages, too.

Asherman syndrome was reported as far back as the end of the nineteenth century. In extreme cases, the entire uterine cavity is obliterated and menstruation may cease. For other women, the scars mean there is insufficient endometrial surface for the fetus to grow healthily.

The scars have come either from intrauterine infection, from D & C procedures (such as is required following a missed abortion), or from late elective abortions (terminations). They occur in as many as 15 percent of women who have had a D & C after a pregnancy but are rare in women having a D & C unassociated with a pregnancy condition.

Once diagnosed by a hysterogram, the scars can be excised by dilating the cervix under general anesthesia and then cutting through the adhesions. This is done with the use of the hysteroscope, which makes each adhesion visible before cutting. An IUD (intrauterine device) is then placed in the uterus, and the patient is put on a course of estrogen, which prevents the adhesions from reforming, for about three months. After that time, the IUD is removed and the patient is advised to try for a pregnancy as quickly as possible.

Fibroids (or fibromyomas) are benign tumors of the muscle and fibrous tissue of the uterine wall. They can be present at different locations in the wall of the uterus: either in the thick middle section of the wall, where they are called intramural; on the surface of the uterus, where they are called subserous, and, in this position, they can be on long stalks and feel separate from the uterus; or, they may be in the depth of the uterine wall and bulge into the uterine cavity, where they are called submucus.

About 40 percent of women, by the age of forty, have fibroids. Remember that they are benign swellings and generally do not require any treatment whatsoever unless they have grown very large in a short space of time, or they cause severe bleeding or pressure in the pelvis. Their role in causing miscarriages has been exaggerated, and they are, in fact, an unusual cause of a miscarriage. Even during a continuing pregnancy, they seldom give any problem, except for some pain if they degenerate. They may cause premature labor if the placenta happens to implant over a fibroid. In general, fibroids, and certainly the small ones, should not be removed surgically in an effort to prevent miscarriage. They are best left alone.

So, abnormalities of the uterus may be responsible for a wide variety of gynecologic disorders, from infertility, to miscarriage, to premature labor, or to hemorrhage following delivery. Or, they may cause none of the above.

How Common Are Uterine Abnormalities as a Cause of Miscarriage?

In the medical literature of the last ten years, research shows that uterine abnormalities account for up to 12 percent of recurrent miscarriages, particularly those that take place between 12 and 24 weeks. Some women with an incompetent cervix may also have an abnormal uterus. Yet surprisingly, considering the extent of some abnormalities, that figure is not high. To look at the figures another way, the majority of women with uterine abnormalities will not experience any reproductive problem.

So do not be upset if, on discovering an anomaly, your doctor decides against aggressive remedies such as corrective surgery. The best method may be to treat you expectantly and deal with an incompetent cervix during your next pregnancy on its merits.

The following story, Annette's, includes a history of a septate uterus. The problems from that cause of miscarriage came after five long and agonizing years of infertility. But, in the end, after much pain and soul-searching, there is a happy ending for Annette and her husband, who now have two delightful little girls.

"I Cried Every Day. I Was Sure I Would Lose the Baby."

It took me five years to achieve my first pregnancy, beginning from the age of twenty-eight. After all these years of being unable to conceive, an infertility specialist helped us. We tried two fertility drugs, Clomid and Pergonal. Then they found one of my tubes was blocked, and I had corrective surgery. Still I did not get pregnant. Next they did sperm antibody tests on both of us, and my husband came up positive. They put him on cortisone for this, to lower his antibody level. A postcoital test done on me, after we had intercourse, showed that the cortisone was working. Four months later I conceived. We were thrilled and, now that I was pregnant, I imagined all my problems were over. I was so excited.

After 8 weeks, I had an ultrasound scan to see how the pregnancy was progressing. They had been checking my hormone levels twice a week from blood tests, and I knew the levels were fine. I was devastated, therefore, to see that the ultrasound showed there was no fetus. It was a blighted ovum, an empty sac. That really broke my heart. I had to stay at the doctor's to have a D & C.

Within another seven to eight months I had conceived again. This time I was put on progesterone suppositories, so we were more hopeful. But at 8 weeks, an ultrasound scan showed another blighted ovum; another empty sac. This time I was recommended to see a different specialist. He encouraged me to try and get pregnant again. So, because of our previous problems with getting pregnant, my husband went back on cortisone. I also started to douche with a solution of baking soda before intercourse. This keeps the acidity of the vagina at a level that makes sperm very active. Using these things we were successful, and I conceived again within three months. Something at least was working.

This time I was placed on vaginal progesterone suppositories from the moment I'd ovulated. When I missed a period, I went for a pregnancy test, not knowing if it was due to being pregnant or because the progesterone could delay the period. I remember that we were leaving the next day for Florida when they told me I was pregnant!

I continued on the progesterone suppositories, which were increased to three a day. For eight weeks, I was advised to be off my feet. I gave up my teaching job for the time and was very, very nervous. I'd kept quiet about the pregnancies and the miscarriages until then. But you can't take off from work because of a fear of miscarriage without letting everyone know. But what if it didn't happen and I had to go back and face them all?

We reached the point of the 8-week ultrasound scan, and there was a heartbeat this time! After the first trimester, I returned to teaching. I was taking progesterone until the 12th week, when the placenta took over progesterone production and I was weaned off the suppositories. An amniocentesis was done at 16 weeks, and the results showed I had a normal pregnancy.

But at about the 5th month, the 22nd week, premature labor started. I felt the uterus contracting and was immediately admitted to the hospital. In the labor room, they attached me to a monitor which records contractions. I was kept in the hospital for three and a half weeks for the control of premature labor.

It was then suspected that I have a septate uterus—that means it's misshapen with a reduced uterine cavity, and, as the pregnancy advances, it cannot expand adequately to accommodate a growing baby. That is why I had problems holding on to the pregnancy. I was kept on high doses of ritodrine to stop my contractions. They also found I had a urinary infection, and I was given antibiotic drugs for that through the IV. Those were probably the hardest three and a half weeks I have ever experienced.

I cried every day. I was sure I'd lose the baby. When my contractions stopped, I was moved off the labor floor to the maternity ward. A special social worker who is involved in helping couples with high-risk pregnancies took me to see the premature babies in the neonatal intensive care unit, so that I could see what happens there in the event it was needed for my baby.

Every minute of every day, I lived with the fear of losing the baby. After those seven years of trying, I felt like I was going crazy. The baby was moving inside of me, and I prayed that if I went into labor now it would survive, knowing that the doctors can do so much with immature babies.

I must have been very difficult, because my doctor turned tough on me. I was moaning and crying a lot, and he came in one day and yelled at me. He told me there were people with cancer coping better than I was. It made me angry. I thought his behavior was inappropriate and insensitive. We've talked about it since, and he explained that sometimes, when dealing with high-risk patients, one has to take that attitude. We wallow in self-pity, which just might make things worse. I don't know. I can't say that was really the best way to handle me.

Basically I'm an upbeat and optimistic person, but after seven years it was just too important to me. Even friends couldn't understand why I persevered. They felt we should adopt a baby. During that time, I became alienated from several of my friends. I resented others for having babies, and some of my friends were on their second and third babies before I'd even achieved my first pregnancy.

Sometimes, it was as though all my friends could talk about was their children. It led to some very miserable times for me. I really felt there was a void in my life. It was with me all the time. We seemed to be going to doctors endlessly. My husband and I had also talked over the possibility of in vitro fertilization. I would have done anything and everything.

But, after that three and a half weeks in the hospital, I was sent home—on complete bed rest. From my 6th to my 8th month, I stayed in bed. I was still taking ritodrine by mouth. Once a week, I went in to see the doctor. But apart from that, I only left my bed to go to the bathroom and maybe sit at the table for lunch. I spent the whole summer in bed! That kind of bed rest is everything you'd imagine it to be. Very very difficult. The days pass so slowly.

Between June and August, I read fifty-two books, every book on the bestseller list, newspapers from cover to cover. A lot of time was spent talking on the phone. What else could I do? It was very hard on my husband, too. He'd bring me breakfast and dinner in bed. We have great friends and they'd come by, bring dinner, and we'd eat together on my bed. But the hardest part was not knowing whether the baby would survive. It was a long, long time of waiting.

As time went by, though, I began to relax. By the 8th month, I'd let myself think that the baby would probably survive if born now. In my 9th month, I was allowed up and to walk around. My pregnancy went to 38 weeks, two weeks before my due date, then I started labor. I'd been warned not necessarily to expect a vaginal delivery, and indeed I had a C-section. But I felt very good immediately afterward. The next day I was up and around. I was absolutely ready to go home and look after my baby.

With our second child, I had similar problems but without such panic as we knew we could get through it. We had no problem conceiving her—they're nineteen months apart. We knew there was the problem with my uterus. Again, I was put on progesterone after ovulation, before a positive pregnancy result. Psychologically, it was a lot easier knowing I could carry to near term and have a healthy baby.

We hired live-in help, so I could keep up the bed rest. I felt more confident and did not need complete bed rest. I would try to spend half the day off my feet. I was back on ritodrine but not on such frequent doses, though until the 8th month I still worried about premature labor. Again, I had a C-section delivery. Now I have two beautiful daughters.

It's been a happy ending, but I wouldn't go through it again! I always wanted two children and my pregnancies were so difficult, taxing, and stressful, that I couldn't put myself, my husband, or my children, through it. Looking back, that whole experience over those seven years really changed me. Until then, I'd felt if I worked hard I could achieve my goals in life. But this was out of my control. I'm the type of person who exercises, eats well, and I take good care of myself. My husband is a lawyer who works hard. But this was something we just couldn't manage as easily as we could other things. I had felt so inadequate during those long years. We came through it with the doctors' help and with special care from a lot of people. I've matured a lot!

What Makes an Incompetent Cervix?

Losing a baby in the second trimester can be a devastating experience, as we read in Paula's story in chapter 1 (page 20). One of the especially sad facts about cervical incompetence is that these women have been losing pregnancies regularly, often at the same week in each pregnancy. Not only is any miscarriage a harrowing experience, but to find yourself repeatedly losing healthy, normal, babies—who, if you could see or hold, look like miniature newborns—then the experience can obviously lead a woman, and her husband, to despair. Later in this chapter we will hear the story of Laura, who has indeed gone through just this type of experience. This is unfortunately a very common problem. But, with new techniques we can now offer much more hope for successful treatment.

The actual incidence of incompetent cervix is unknown but is thought to be about 1 to 2 percent of normal deliveries. It has been estimated that an incompetent cervix is the cause of up to one-fifth of late miscarriages (that is, those following the 12th week).

Technically speaking, a cervix is classified as incompetent if it fails to maintain an intrauterine pregnancy to term. The cervix begins to dilate far too early and easily, the amniotic membranes push through, and, following either a dramatic rupture of the membranes or blood loss, you go into a rapid, short premature labor. The baby is then born too early for independent life. Only recently have doctors fully understood just what can happen to the cervix. Although the procedure of inserting a stitch to hold the cervix closed has been in practice since 1951, we are now more competent in diagnosing and treating the condition successfully.

Normally, the cervix acts as the plug that holds the pregnancy in place. The cervix is mainly composed of collagen, or connective tissue, and only 10 percent of it is muscle. When you are not pregnant the cervix is rigid, fibrous, and hard. But it softens during pregnancy, an action known as "ripening," and that is probably caused by the action of the pregnancy hormones. If the cervix ripens too early, the pregnancy can be pushed through a weakened cervix from about the 14th to the 20th week.

All too often the cervix has been affected prior to the pregnancy by trauma, for example, from previous D & C's or elective terminations of pregnancy. Until recently no one realized how gingerly the cervix should be treated. For example, one method of treatment for painful periods used to be dilating, or overstretching, the cervix, which usually tore the muscle fibers and led to incompetence. This treatment is now unnecessary because of the availability of effective medications. With our increased medical knowledge, there is no reason why induced abortions (terminations) should now result in incompetent cervix.

If an abortion is needed after the 10th or 11th week, when the cervix would otherwise have to be opened, or dilated, unduly, your doctor does not have to use metal dilators that can tear and damage the cervix. Instead, the cervix can be ripened, or softened, using *laminaria* (seaweed) sticks, which are inserted into the cervix and left overnight before the procedure. The risks of mechanical trauma and damage to the cervix can thus be obviated.

The cervix can unfortunately also be damaged in childbirth, torn either by the passage of the infant during delivery or by instruments such as forceps or a vacuum extractor. The other major cause of an incompetent cervix, as we discussed in the previous section, is uterine abnormalities, which, by preventing expansion of the top of the uterus as the pregnancy grows, force the cervix to open below.

A diagnosis of incompetent cervix can be made from a combination of your personal medical history, which is most important, and an internal examination. Shortly after your last period ends and you know you're not pregnant, if your doctor can pass a finger through the cervix into the uterine cavity, or if he can pass a size 6 Hegar dilator through the cervical canal, then he would strongly suspect such a diagnosis.

Hysterography, described in the previous section, can also be used for diagnosis. The dye may spill back around the instrument that has been placed in the cervix and through which the dye is injected, to show the width of the cervix. Ultrasound, in expert hands, can also be used for diagnosis of incompetent cervix, especially if you are already pregnant. On the screen, you may be able to see a widely dilated cervix, with membranes and amniotic fluid bulging down. With use of the newly introduced transvaginal ultrasound, more is being learned about diagnosing abnormalities of the cervix.

The main indication of a weak cervix, however, remains a past history of recurrent miscarriages between 14 and 24 weeks. Usually there will have been little heavy bleeding; the membranes may even have ruptured before any contractions were felt. The contractions that do come are short and usually quite painless. The fetus is often, very sadly, born alive.

Prevention of Damage to the Cervix

Doctors treat D & C procedures with caution. They are aware that any woman in her reproductive years should not have her cervix forcibly dilated beyond Hegar 8 millimeters, to prevent tearing of the cervical fibers.

If you are in need of an advanced induced abortion, your doctor will probably ripen the cervix the night before, using the seaweed (laminaria) I described earlier, or by placing prostaglandins in the vagina, which also ripen the cervix overnight. They then do not have to do much dilatation (the D part of the D & C) because you will already have been dilated.

If you receive word of an abnormal pap smear that may eventually need to be treated, cryosurgery (freezing) or laser therapy may be used, rather than a surgical cone biopsy, where some of the cervix is cut away, which may lead to incompetence. So your doctor now has the alternative of these newer methods that can be used with less trauma to the cervix and which are just as effective.

At medical schools, young doctors in training are being taught such methods of *prevention* of illness, at the same time as they are discussing methods of treatment. This new attitude runs through all areas of medicine.

Cerclage, McDonald Suture, or the Shirodkar Stitch

The placing of a stitch into the cervix to tighten and close it is the method of treatment for an incompetent, or weak, cervix. The procedure was described just over thirty years ago. Putting in the stitch is often also called a Shirodkar, but that name, in fact, only applies to one particular method. Professor Shirodkar was an eminent physician to whom many women are grateful, as his method has helped maintain so many pregnancies in the uterus.

See Figure 9, which shows the site of placement of the suture to close the cervix.

Why Does an Incompetent Cervix Give Way from 12 to 14 Weeks On?

In the previous section, I mentioned that the cervix is made up of only about 10 percent muscle; the rest of it is a fibrous material that can stretch and soften in pregnancy. The cervix

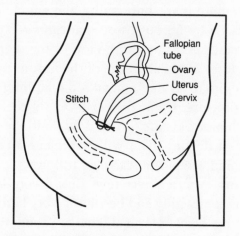

Figure 9. This diagram illustrates the placement of the cervical stitch.

opens at ovulation allowing the entrance of sperm, but apart from that time it is normally closed.

During pregnancy, the cervix softens slightly, but otherwise it remains tight and is filled with a very thick or viscid mucus plug that stays in place until very late in pregnancy. At that point the cervix starts to shorten, or efface, because it is beginning to open so the baby's head can go through it. The cervix must remain tightly closed to protect the fetus and uterine contents from the introduction of infection from the outside or the vagina.

The part of the uterus above the cervix is made up mainly of strong muscle. During early pregnancy, the uterus increases in size due to pregnancy hormones, which cause muscle fibers in the body of the uterus to increase in number and to lengthen. Then, from the middle of the second trimester, about the 12th to 14th week on, the uterus also gets bigger because the growing fetus and amniotic sac now push up and cause its expansion. This is what normally happens before delivery. The uterus gets large, and at around 40 weeks, the strong muscle helps expel the baby through the cervical opening.

However, if the cervix is weak, or incompetent, or if the uterus is misshapen, this normal sequence of events does not occur. When there is an abnormality, the muscle in the uterus is often replaced by fibrous tissue that cannot expand. As the baby grows and pushes up on the top of the uterus (fundus), the uterus refuses to give because of the fibrous tissue, and the pregnancy begins to act like a metal rod—pushing down on the cervix. This pressure begins around 14 to 16 weeks. The membranes and amniotic sac are forced down into the weak cervix, which will start dilating. This will precipitate a rupture of the membranes, and a rapid miscarriage follows.

Symptoms are often very few. But, if you do notice that your uterus is contracting and becoming very hard at this time, if there is a very heavy mucus discharge or any vaginal bleeding, you should report to your doctor. Often no pain is experienced until the miscarriage is already well advanced. However, pressure on the cervix may produce a pain in the vagina that has been described as "like a knife pushing upward from the vagina into the pelvis." Severe backache may also occur. Any such symptoms around this time of pregnancy should be immediately reported.

However, if a diagnosis has been made and a stitch can be put in at the correct time, the success rate for producing a healthy term baby is very good, at least 80 to 90 percent. New studies have shown that the earlier in pregnancy the stitch is put in, and the higher up on the cervix your doctor can place it, the more effective is its hold. You and your doctor will be doing your best to simulate nature. The cervix needs to be closed and tight to maintain a pregnancy.

Sometimes an incompetent cervix, especially one that happens beyond about 20 weeks, may be associated with uterine contractions. It is not known whether this is true premature labor, or whether the weak cervix is causing the contractions. Nevertheless, at this late stage in addition to the stitch, your doctor may put you on the drug *ritodrine* to prevent further contractions. The drug is safe to take in pregnancy; its only side effect on you is a rapid heart beat. It has been approved by the Food and Drug Administration (FDA) for use in the United States for the past four to five years, even though it has been used in Europe and other parts of the world for at least twice that length of time. It only has FDA approval for use in pregnancy once the 20-week stage of pregnancy has been attained.

How the Shirodkar or McDonald Stitch Is Put In

The term *cerclage* can also be used to describe the procedure. It aptly describes the method whereby a stitch is placed around the cervix, making it much like a tobacco pouch where the strings have been pulled tight. In the same way, the stitch pulls the cervix tight. This famous technique, as mentioned earlier, is named after one of its main proponents, Professor Shirodkar. His was just one technique and, as it is quite a lengthy procedure, it is often not done quite as he described it. Other doctors have lent their names to similar techniques, such as the Macdonald or Lash procedures. They are all modifications of the same idea, tying the strings or tape in different ways. The tape can even be tied through a button to prevent it from loosening and rolling down the cervix.

A most important point to bear in mind is that the stitch should be put in *early.* It used to be said that it could not be placed before about the 14th week of pregnancy. But that late date was dictated by the fact that, prior to the use of ultrasound, neither the doctor nor the patient would have heard the fetal heartbeat, or felt movement, until that time. Now, sonography can tell us if the fetus is alive from 6 weeks or even earlier. Obviously, one would not want to put in a stitch if there was not a live pregnancy in the uterus.

I often recommend putting in the stitch around 9 to 10 weeks. The earlier the stitch is in, the longer it may hold the pregnancy. One of the reasons is that while the cervix is still as long as it is going to be, it gives the doctor more to work with. And the stitch is placed as *high* up in the cervix as possible. Throughout pregnancy, the cervix normally contracts because it contains muscle tissue. This may cause the stitch to dislodge, and so it must be put in high and firmly.

If there are any overwhelming high-risk factors, and you are unsure of the health of the fetus, you can have a chorionic villus sampling (CVS) test between the 6th and 9th week, which is a very early method of providing the information usually discovered by amniocentesis. (See chapter 7, page 176, for more on these two methods.) The CVS can precede putting in the stitch, which will be done once normal results are obtained.

Generally, the stitch should not be put in if you are actively bleeding or contracting, as the procedure may mask what is going to be an *inevitable* miscarriage.

A stitch can even be placed in the cervix *before* you undertake a pregnancy. Usually this is only done where there is virtually no cervix present, making it technically very difficult or impossible to insert one once the patient has become pregnant and the cervix has already begun to shorten. It is quite rare to do this, because putting a stitch in between pregnancies might interfere with fertility, and the technique used would almost inevitably mean a C-section delivery. As the type of cerclage technique will vary from patient to patient, you must rely on your doctor's advice.

When your physician has decided that a stitch is needed, it will be done in the hospital. Prior to putting in the stitch, an ultrasound scan will be done to ensure that the fetus is alive (its heart is beating) and there are no other problems. You will be admitted into the hospital either on the day of the procedure or possibly the night before. Some anesthesia will be necessary as it is a little too painful otherwise. An epidural anesthetic, which is often used during labor, is a common choice. The procedure is done in the operating room. Your legs are placed in stirrups, and the technique usually takes about fifteen to thirty minutes. Following the procedure you may be discharged home on the same day or kept in overnight. The fetal heartbeat can be checked afterward by ultrasound or possibly with a Fetone.

Treatment and Care After Surgery

Once a stitch is put in, the doctor keeps a close eye on the patient, as accidents can happen to the stitch itself: the knot may come loose, or the stitch can roll down the cervix and loosen. It is very important to see the doctor regularly, even once a week initially, until the fetus is viable at around 30 to 32 weeks.

You will probably have to be examined vaginally at each visit, as your doctor will want to know how secure the stitch is. If it has rolled down or if the cervix is beginning to open, your doctor may even decide to put in another stitch.

He may advise some bed rest after the procedure, because gravity can put pressure on the cervix.

As the stitch is a foreign body, it could be a site for infection. So, as a preventive measure, one week out of every month I may prescribe an antibiotic, either by mouth or vaginally, to prevent infection. This is not always done and depends on the particular patient's history.

I have always believed in seeing patients with a history of miscarriage often and in giving a lot of reassurance. I believe this has a physically beneficial effect.

What if You Have Contractions Even with the Stitch in Place?

One common fear among women needing a cervical stitch is whether intercourse is safe, even after a stitch, or whether it will set off contractions. If you feel comfortable about the idea and your doctor feels there is no inherent danger, then he may tell you it is safe to resume intercourse. But you will probably be asked to use a condom to avoid the possible effects of the prostaglandins from semen, which just might stimulate uterine contractions, and to minimize infection.

If premature labor does begin, ritodrine may be given as treatment. As I mentioned earlier, ritodrine is only approved for use from the 20th week. However, even with no signs of premature labor, if a patient is very high-risk and anxious, I sometimes give her ritodrine from 20 weeks. A side effect, as I mentioned earlier, is that it will make your heart beat faster, but it does not have adverse fetal effects.

When Is the Stitch Removed?

The stitch can be taken out in the doctor's office and does not usually require hospitalization or an anesthetic. Removal is not painful. We aim for two weeks before due date, or the 38th week. Once this stage is reached the baby is fully mature and the stitch can safely be removed.

You would not want to go into labor with the stitch in because this could lead to a frantic rush to get it out in time, and delivery with the stitch in place could lead to bad tearing of the cervix. You also need a few days to allow any infection from the stitch site to leave your body. These are the reasons why we always try to remove the stitch before labor begins.

After the stitch is removed, it is common to have minimal bright bleeding from the stitch site. Labor itself usually starts within hours or one to two days, especially if the cervix is very weak. However, labor may even be delayed *beyond* term in some cases, possibly because of scarring from the stitch site!

Treatment of Another Uterine Problem: Fibroids

Surgery for fibroids? *Fibromyomas,* the technical name for fibroids, are common in women of childbearing age, especially as they get older. As many as 40 percent of women by the age of forty have these benign muscle tumors. In nonpregnant women, fibroids may cause excessively heavy periods and discomfort from pressure. But in pregnancy they are in fact *not* a major cause of miscarriage, and a doctor would not terminate a pregnancy just because of small fibroids.

As mentioned earlier, fibroids can occur in different parts of the uterus and the uterine wall. What has emerged as a fairly common problem these days is that women in their late thirties have had time to develop fibroids, sometimes as big as a large melon. In the nonpregnant state this could make you look as though you were 5 months pregnant! The question then is whether you should get pregnant with the fibroids, or have them removed first.

My feeling is that it is probably best for you to undertake a pregnancy first—and see what happens. This may sound cruel, especially after all my previous comments about the trauma of a miscarriage. But, you may not miscarry even with the fibroids, in which case you will have discovered to your fortune that the fibroids were not a problem. Should you, unfortunately, mis-carry—at least you know that surgery for removal of the fi-broids, a myomectomy, is probably necessary. It is not an operation ever to be undertaken lightly, as removing large multiple fibroids might leave a severely scarred uterus. This scarring could even affect your fertility. Also, if during removal of fibroids, the cavity of the uterus is entered, a C-section delivery will be needed in your next pregnancy to avoid uterine rupture.

This is why I feel it is better to try a pregnancy first, before undertaking any surgery, unless your doctor advises otherwise in your particular case. Fibroids may soften during pregnancy. That process might cause some pain and occasionally a low-grade fever, but it can be overcome with bed rest and a mild painkiller such as Tylenol.

Another potential problem with a large fibroid or fibroids is the implantation of the placenta over one of the tumors, which could cause premature labor. This is a treatable condi-tion. Occasionally, very rarely, a fibroid obstructs the pelvic outlet, and you might need to be delivered by C-section.

Fibroids also should not be removed from the uterus *dur-ing* a pregnancy or at the time of a C-section, as the procedure may be accompanied by severe hemorrhage. However, you must leave this decision to your obstetrician.

But now let me bring in Laura's story, to share with you some of the pain and heartache of second trimester miscar-riages from an incompetent cervix. Three times she had lost a pregnancy at 20 weeks, but she then had a successful pregnancy after a stitch was placed around her cervix.

"The Doctor Gave Me the Confidence to Try Again."

My son was born when I was twenty-six. I felt very strong during my pregnancy and worked up to three weeks before he was born. About five years later I decided I wanted another child. And both my husband and I were very happy when I became pregnant. Everything was going fine at first with this second pregnancy. I did all the usual things. But I remember, one day, I shopped and started cooking at home, when suddenly I began to feel very bad cramps. I didn't know what was happening. I was about 20 weeks pregnant at the time.

I'd never had a miscarriage before, so the experience was very frightening. I was alone in the house. I decided to lie down, hoping it would just turn out to be gas pains. But the cramps grew worse. Eventually, I called an ambulance to take me to the hospital. I was rushed to emergency, where I had very good doctors. I desperately wanted this baby to be saved. But my doctor warned me I'd go into labor and that I would be given a shot of painkiller to help me along, because it was unlikely the baby would be born alive.

Labor was a terrible experience because, as you are going through the pain of contractions, you're holding back—to stop the fetus coming. When he was born, his lungs were not fully developed and he died. I had a glimpse of the baby, but there was no chance to hold him. Afterward I was very depressed. I didn't know how to deal with it. I went back to work as soon as possible. My son, who was then six years old, was very concerned. My husband wanted us to try again, but I was afraid. We waited another two years before I decided I could brave another pregnancy. I became pregnant easily. At least I've had no problems on that score.

The doctor explained I'd have a stitch put in and that I'd have to rest a lot. I worked up to the second month, but after the stitch was put in I gave up going to the office and stayed home—in bed most of the time. Luckily I was able to do some written work for my job from home.

One evening, I felt like cooking for my family. My husband had been doing most of the housework, and I was sorry for him. So I got up and began puttering about the kitchen. Later that same evening, I began staining. My husband rushed me to the hospital. Things seemed fine, so we came back home. Eventually the staining stopped. But three or four days later a lot of fluid leaked. Again it was around the 20-week stage.

I went back to the hospital, where I was kept under observation. They said I had lost a lot of amniotic fluid, but that the baby was still alive. They hoped that the amniotic fluid level would refill itself.

All that time in the hospital it was like being on a seesaw. One day everything was fine, they all had great hopes for the baby. The next day, things would suddenly change. I began to run a fever. As there was a danger of infection, they suggested inducing labor. But I begged them to wait until the very last minute. Finally, though, I began to run a very high fever and labor started. When I went into labor, I just wanted to die. "Why is this happening to me?" I kept saying. "I'm not a bad person." The stitch was unfortunately still in place and labor was very painful. The nurses were being supportive, but the pain was unbearable until the surgeon arrived to take out the stitch.

This baby was born alive. She lived for forty-five minutes. They brought her to me, wrapped up. And they put her in my arms. I could see her face, touch her fingers and her hair. Her eyes were closed, but her face was fully formed. And she had very, very long fingers. It was a Catholic hospital, and I have to say they treated the whole nightmare experience with utmost respect, which I thank them for. They had already named and baptized her. Even that gave me a sense of peace. My consolation was in being able to hold her. I felt much better than I had after I lost the first pregnancy.

But, afterward, I went into an even greater depression, which lasted a lot longer. My husband was helpful, understanding, and supportive, but nothing would shift my mood. We went on vacation to Puerto Rico, but even then, five months after losing the baby, I still used to burst into tears. Then I'd feel guilty for my husband's and son's sakes. I could never get rid of the guilt that if I hadn't got up that day, maybe I would not have lost her.

Once back home, I could see that this time the depression had affected my son, who was then nine years old. He was worried that if I became pregnant again, he'd lose me. My husband suggested adopting a baby and I agreed to the idea. But, as the months went by, we decided we would give pregnancy one more try.

So I became pregnant again, and this time I felt I was well prepared. The stitch was put in much earlier, and I stayed home and rested. But, again around the same time, I felt the fluid leaking. Again, I was rushed to emergency. The amniotic sac appeared only to be leaking, and they felt it would close naturally. I stayed in the hospital for five days, again holding onto all hope. But I lost this pregnancy too—it was a boy.

But, before I lost the third pregnancy, a girlfriend—who had lost two babies and then had finally given birth first to a little girl and then a boy—had given me the name of a miscarriage specialist.

I kept that phone number without doing anything, for about a year. My husband said he wouldn't rush me but would wait till I was ready to try again.

In the end, I did call the specialist. We both went in to see him, and he ran some tests on us. I was sent for blood tests. An X ray was taken of my uterus. I was told I have an incompetent cervix. Next time I became pregnant he said he would put in a stitch *much* earlier, between 8 and 10 weeks, and he would put me on medication (ritodrine) to relax the uterus just as soon as was possible. I would also have to stay in bed as much as possible.

He gave me the confidence to try again. After all those years of miscarriages—I was then thirty-nine years old—I felt that if it didn't work this time, it was going to be the last time for me. Can you imagine our joy, then, when this last pregnancy was all right? I had the stitch as planned, and I went near to term—and now have a lovely little girl, just two weeks old today! A miracle baby.

With my first pregnancy I had become pregnant accidentally. I did everything "wrong." I shopped, I cleaned, I went to work. It never occurred to me to take care. The day before I went into labor, I walked forty blocks in the August heat! The following day, my waters broke and I went into labor right away. I was taken straight to the labor room and gave birth two and a half hours later. It never dawned on me for a second I'd have problems in the future.

With this last pregnancy, I had a stitch placed in my cervix and stayed in bed for months. I followed the doctor's suggestions to the letter. I still can't believe we went through it all. What kept me going was the feeling that if it was God's will for me not to have a baby, why did I get pregnant so easily? And each baby that has been born was seen to be healthy. There was nothing chromosomally wrong with them. They were not abnormal. The problem was with my cervix, which we overcame—with help of a cerclage.

5

Is There a Mismatch Between You and Your Partner and the Baby?

Whchuk **HEN YOU ARE happily** pregnant, nurturing the unborn in your swelling abdomen, nothing could seem further from your own particular reality than that you might in fact be attempting to reject it. For most women, the very thought of rejecting the fetus would be an anathema. They love their partners; they very much want a child; so how could they, of all people, be rejecting this desperately wanted baby? But, your body may in fact be reacting to foreign tissue; in what, outside of pregnancy, would be considered a very normal manner.

Do be reassured in this chapter on the effects of the body's autoimmune system in pregnancy that I am not talking about psychogenic issues. If you have an immunologic problem, no amount of positive thinking, no amount of stress reduction and bed rest would alone overcome the condition.

Let me also reassure you that with the fear of AIDS which permeates our time, the word *immune* can trigger negative feelings in many women's minds. The immune system is indeed extremely important in keeping us healthy and strong. But the

126

immunological problems I shall describe do not bear any relationship to the virus-induced breakdown in immune protection that has so devastated our society.

This fascinating high-tech field of immunology—within the realm of miscarriage research—has already helped many hundreds of women (and their partners). The type of woman offered testing, to see if she does have immunological problems, is the classic repeated early miscarrier for whom no "obvious" cause can be found.

It is now thought that possibly one-third or more of recurrent miscarriers are affected, which means that many women may be eligible for this type of help. However, the treatment is still considered controversial and experimental. Nevertheless, the statistics emerging from major research centers show success rates of 75 to 90 percent. Indeed, respected experts on miscarriage now believe this will soon be accepted as an important known cause of and treatment for recurrent miscarriage.

For women who have given up hope, these figures, as you can imagine, are very encouraging, and waiting lists are growing.

What Is the Immunological Problem?

Scientists have long had to grapple with the fact that it is less surprising that some pregnant women reject their fetuses than that any fetus, in fact, makes it through to full-term birth. Why? Because the processes of conception, fertilization, and embryological development go against one of the basic tenets of nature: The body, as transplant surgeons well know, rejects anything it does not recognize as its own. The embryo is only 50 percent its mother's tissue; the other half, which comes from the father, is considered by her body to be foreign tissue.

In the very early days following conception, the *trophoblast,* the bundle of fetal cells of the developing embryo and placenta, actually comes in contact with the mother's tissue and her blood as it attaches to the uterine wall. The mother's blood cells make antibodies to this partly "foreign" tissue, as would be expected.

Normally, however, a pregnant woman will also make *special* antibodies that mask and protect these trophoblast cells from the antibodies formed. These special antibodies, peculiar to the pregnant state, are known as *blocking antibodies*. (See Figure 10.)

The precedent to this type of research was found in the world of kidney transplants. Doctors, struggling to find ways to encourage their patients to accept a donor kidney, found their tolerance was increased if they had previously had a blood transfusion.

A woman who becomes pregnant has naturally been exposed to her partner's foreign cells through intercourse. Semen carries some tissue proteins, called antigens (that is, proteins that trigger an antibody response). It doesn't matter how many times you have had intercourse previously; even once is enough to expose you to antigens that help produce the protective blocking antibody. But some women's bodies just do not recognize their partner's tissue as foreign enough.

Doctors used to think that in pregnancy the immune system was suppressed. In fact, in a curious reversal of normal situations, it is the *underactive* immune system not recognizing this tissue as foreign that prevents the "blocking antibody" from being made, not, as you might imagine, a wildly aggressive immune system attacking all foreign tissue at will. It is now believed that certain men and women are genetically too similar (though if your husband had to donate his kidney to you, the similarity would have its advantages). In this case, the woman adopts the husband's antigens as her own.

There is no way of knowing beforehand who will be affected, though it does lend credibility to the Biblical juncture against marrying a first cousin or a very close relative. The problem is "asymptomatic," meaning you have no symptoms such as a high temperature or nausea. And how much you love your partner bears not the slightest relevance. From studies, it

Between mother and child, a fragile barrier

Trophoblast cells, which form the layer between the uterus and the placenta, are arranged in tiny, tree-shaped projections known early in pregnancy as chorionic villi. It is the only fetal tissue that comes into contact with the mother. The trophoblast cells are selective in what they let through. For example, they allow some but not all of the plasma constituents to pass, and no cells.

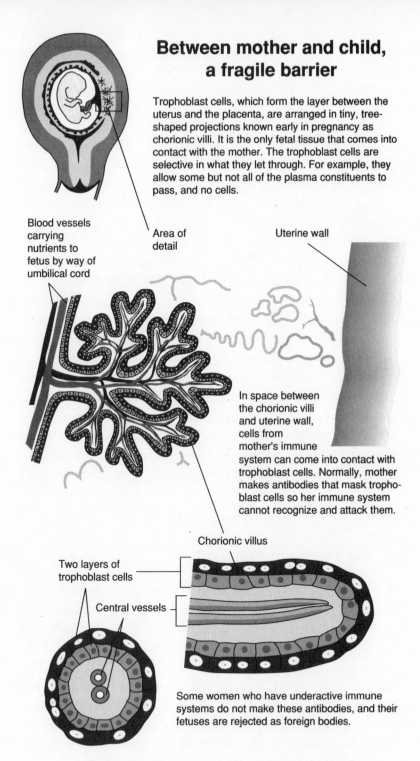

Blood vessels carrying nutrients to fetus by way of umbilical cord

Area of detail

Uterine wall

In space between the chorionic villi and uterine wall, cells from mother's immune system can come into contact with trophoblast cells. Normally, mother makes antibodies that mask trophoblast cells so her immune system cannot recognize and attack them.

Chorionic villus

Two layers of trophoblast cells

Central vessels

Some women who have underactive immune systems do not make these antibodies, and their fetuses are rejected as foreign bodies.

Figure 10. Blocking antibodies and trophoblast cells.

129

has been found that there is a 1 percent chance, in a randomly selected sample of couples, that you will share major antigens.

In the mid seventies, researchers began to detect the "blocking factor" in pregnant women. Research on this subject was begun both in Britain and the United States. Dr. Mowbray at Saint Mary's Hospital, in London, began testing women, and then immunizing them with their own white blood cells or with their partner's. At least twice as many women who had previously miscarried more than three times went on to have full-term babies if they had been injected with their partner's white blood cells. Here in the United States, Dr. Alan Beer, in Chicago, and Dr. Susan Cowchock, of Jefferson Medical College, Philadelphia, have also made great strides in research. With this technique the success rates vary, but there is at least a 75 percent success rate for women who have had between three and six previous miscarriages. Women with successful pregnancies were studied, and one could see that, by comparison, women who were miscarrying lacked a certain substance called blocking factor that could be detected in the blood. White cell immunization treatment may increase amounts of blocking antibody or stimulate protective immune suppressor cells in order to help the pregnancy survive.

How Will You Be Immunized?

Our white blood cells are the centers of antibody manufacture. In pregnancy, the mother has only a weakened version of her partner's proteins inside her. Injection with *his* white blood cells, usually before pregnancy, will mean she has the full force to work with. "Immunized" is in fact a misleading term. The mother is "stimulated" by an injection of her husband's antigens to produce the blocking factor. If you are already pregnant when the results of the blood test are obtained, you can be immunized while pregnant. Or, if you have just miscarried, then the treatment can be given soon afterward.

With the injection, you will notice no side effects other

than maybe a little swelling on the arm where drops of the white blood cells are placed. You will then be tested for its effectiveness, that is, to see if you have produced antibodies. Then, if you are not pregnant, and if you do not conceive for more than six months, you may have to be re-tested and perhaps be given a repeat treatment.

If a woman proves to be too close still to her husband's antigens, or if he is an unsuitable donor, then white blood cells from an unrelated donor can be injected. Because of the current AIDS scare, many are fearful of taking a stranger's white blood cells. As a result, plasma from semen is now sterilized and rendered free of viruses. At another center, blood cells from human placentas are used.

The treatment is available right now at only eight centers in the United States (and at about thirty centers worldwide). The procedure is improving all the time, particularly in the screening methods used to determine which couples are eligible. The treatment has also been found to be more successful if you have never had a full-term pregnancy before.

The method, however, is still controversial and continues to be regarded by some people (including insurers) as experimental.

As is the case with treatment for an incompetent cervix, this high-tech immunization treatment cannot be given to a patient, who is then sent home to hope for the best. Such patients require a lot of medical supervision and, of course, sympathy and understanding. Having lost several pregnancies already, they will be anxious until their baby is born.

Won't the Injection of White Blood Cells Harm the Baby?

No one can yet know for sure. You will be taking an element of risk because the program has not yet been fully tested over time. To guard against problems, you should only be treated at a center where research is actively being carried out. Infants have been followed up, at centers worldwide, for the last six to seven years. From Dr. Cowchock's center in Philadelphia, where many babies have been born using this method, only two have shown medical problems that may be related to the treatment.

Whether these children developed problems because of their mother's immunological therapy, or despite it, is an unknown. In fact, no studies have shown an increase in congenital abnormalities in the offspring of patients receiving this treatment. However, many well-informed couples, aware of the minimal risk involved, are eager to take up the treatment, since it offers them hope of having their own baby.

Who Can It Help?

Rachel is typical of many women who ultimately have found salvation through the immunization technique. Previously, she had undergone four miscarriages, all of which seemed to occur for no obvious reason. The experience of these recurring losses, and the build-up of fear and anxiety, led Rachel to a state of extreme nervousness. Atypically, Rachel is young for this type of treatment; she was then still under age thirty. Yet, why should she have waited any longer?

Immunization and prolonged bed rest have produced a healthy and beautiful baby for Rachel and her husband. But the pregnancy, as you will see, was not uneventful.

"Now It Was My Fourth Miscarriage and I Wanted to Know Why It Was Happening to Me."

My first pregnancy was three and a half years ago, when I was twenty-five years old. I had no problems at all in getting pregnant, and my husband and I were thrilled. I never imagined anything would go wrong. The pregnancy went nearly three months, then during one of my visits to the doctor, he saw no heartbeat on the sonogram. I wasn't staining and had felt no cramps. I genuinely thought my doctor was making a mistake. The baby had grown to 12 weeks. What could have gone wrong? But I had the D & C there in his office because otherwise, I was warned, I might miscarry over the weekend and end up as an emergency case.

I did a lot of crying and felt very depressed. But, knowing I had been very nauseated throughout the past three months, I decided maybe it hadn't been right all along. My doctor told me a lot of people miscarry the first time, so he recommended no testing. He also said to wait three months. Well, those three months were unbearable. I ran over in my mind everything I thought I'd done wrong. We'd been away, so maybe it was the flying? Maybe I shouldn't have made the bed. As I said, I did a lot of crying. I'd be making dinner and start to cry. The only thing that helped me was going back to work.

I didn't want to wait, but those three months passed, and then we tried again. I became pregnant, but I lost this one after four weeks. I hadn't even gotten to my first doctor's appointment. I had a positive pregnancy test and then I started staining at home. I got into bed and put my feet up. But I lost it at home on a Saturday night. I was bleeding heavily, with a lot of cramps. We saved everything we could. Then I waited till 7:30 A.M. to call the doctor. He said, "Maybe you didn't lose the pregnancy." But I knew I had, because after a large clot came out the bleeding stopped. It was still the weekend, and the doctor said to come in and see him on Monday. That whole day of waiting was very traumatic.

But when he looked at the sonogram, the doctor said, "You're right, you lost the baby!" It meant another D & C. Now it was my second miscarriage and I wanted to know why it was happening to me. I kept asking him, "Should I quit my job? Should I be off my feet?" But his attitude was, "there is little that can be done until you've lost three." My doctor said he'd put me on progesterone and thyroid medication the next time around.

The third time, I got pregnant again very easily. But this time I really took care. I even drank a lot of milk! In my job, where I work with learning disabled children, who can be very emotionally demanding, I made sure I lifted no one. I would stay off my feet from 3:00 P.M. till the next morning. I was on proges-

terone from the time of my pregnancy test, and multivitamins.
But I was a nervous wreck. The doctor did an ultrasound earlier
this time. But, although I was so very very careful, I again started
staining at home. I went into the doctor and he said it didn't look
good on the ultrasound. He had to do a D & C again. They did
try to test the chromosomes of the fetus, but they couldn't get the
cells to grow. My husband and I went for genetic counseling and
we were both normal. My doctor suggested that next time he
would increase the progesterone levels and begin the treatment
earlier.

I returned to work, and at least the children there were very
loving to me. But on my drive home from work I'd cry my eyes
out. My husband kept saying I should see someone for depression.
I did call Resolve in New York, but their group meetings were a
long way from where we were living, and I felt that making all that
effort might make me feel worse.

Friends all began offering me names of different doctors to try.
But I didn't know which one to choose. My own doctor did not
treat me any differently. All he kept saying was, "You'll have a
baby, don't worry. You're young."

I'd talked to my husband about applying for adoption. In fact,
I did put my name down with a couple of agencies. We both hoped
that the old trick of having the reassurance of your name down with
an agency would help us with our own child.

Then I became pregnant for the fourth time. It lasted about
two months, when I started staining. An ultrasound scan showed
again there was no heartbeat. The doctor had been testing my
blood for progesterone levels, and I had previously been warned
that the pregnancy was not growing as well as it should be.

At that point, I made an appointment to see a specialist. He
was very kind and treated me sympathetically. He made a chart of
all the things he would do, the kinds of tests that could be run. He
even mentioned immunology. Three or four tests were done right
away, plus one on my husband. An endometrial biopsy was arranged. Once those results were obtained, we were tested to see
whether we would be candidates for immunization.

That was all quite dramatic because my husband hates needles.
And endless blood tests are taken. We went again to my doctor's
office and our blood was sent overnight to Philadelphia. We were
found to be eligible for the immunization procedure and finally
went to Philadelphia for it. More blood tests were done on both

of us, plus an AIDS screening test on my husband's blood as it was to be transfused into me. The next morning, they took a pint of my husband's blood. Then we spent the day like tourists wandering around Philadelphia. Later in the afternoon, a needleful of his white blood cells was injected into me. It was a clear white liquid. The doctor put four drops onto little spots on my skin, and the rest was injected into a vein. A rash developed on the skin and it was itchy as I'd been warned. We were told that if we could get pregnant within a month, then we would have a 75 percent chance of a healthy normal pregnancy. If conception took much longer, we might have to repeat the process.

After that I became a nervous wreck. There was the very real pressure of getting pregnant. I found that I shouted at my husband if he was not home on time on "the day." I became obsessed by getting pregnant and bought an ovulation predictor kit. Eventually, I went to see the specialist early, about a vaginal infection. He suggested doing a pregnancy test right then.

When the nurse turned around and cried out that it was positive, I was over the moon. It seemed as though they were all thrilled for me at the specialist's office, even though they hardly knew me. What a difference that atmosphere made! Then the specialist told me to go home and get as much rest as possible. I called my job and told them I would not be coming in—maybe not returning at all—as I was going to be off for months. And then, we hoped, I would have a baby!

The bed rest was tough. I was nervous most of the day. I moved into my mother's house, so there would be company. My husband was excellent and very supportive. But I worried about everything. If I got up too many times to go to the bathroom, or went down the stairs because I was hungry, and there was no one around, was I doing too much? In this situation, you tend to double-think everything. I was also scared because I didn't have a job to go back to. What if I lost the baby and had to look for a new job? I would be doubly upset.

The days were very long. I slept a lot. From the sixth week to the third month, I was also very sick. Although I'd been told that was normal, still I worried about its effect. If my breasts weren't as tender as they'd been the day before, I would panic. I must have called the doctor's office four days a week with my questions and problems. They were very good to me. If they felt unsure from my questions, they would tell me to come in for an ultrasound scan.

Once we could see the heartbeat on the sonogram, I felt much better. But it was traumatic, because I had twenty-four hours a day in which to think and to worry.

Two months into the pregnancy, once again I started staining and I became hysterical. The doctor increased the progesterone dosage and told my husband to give me a glass of wine to calm me down. As I hadn't been drinking any alcohol, it in fact knocked me right out and I slept for hours! I did stop staining and later went for another ultrasound. Everything was fine. I went home and *really* put my feet up this time.

Then there was the question of amniocentesis. Should we take the risk of the test, when we were so desperate to have this baby? That was a tough decision. We'd done everything for five pregnancies to keep the babies, and now I would be taking a 1 in 400 chance of the amniocentesis causing a miscarriage. But, I really didn't want to bring a child into the world with terrible problems. My work is with special education children, and I know how hard they can be.

By the 5th month, my doctor said I could start resting less, maybe even go out for dinner. So I began to go downstairs for the evening meal, to join my husband and my parents. Two months later, I allowed myself to go out for dinner. We went out a couple of times. Just to prove that a healthy pregnancy is not as easy to lose as I'd feared, we were even involved in an automobile accident on one of those occasions—and I was fine.

I didn't go out to dinner again, but I spent more time on my feet at home. In the end, I went ten days past term. The doctor was seeing me twice a week by then. He remained kind, helpful, and reassuring. I was having regular nonstress tests on the fetal monitor because the baby seemed to move less. Then, on a Sunday morning, I started staining with very small cramps. I knew this was labor starting. He was born later that night and was a healthy 8 pounds 7 ounces.

I still cannot believe it. After all this, he's here! He's mine. . . . I stand for hours watching him sleep.

Ultimately whether the successful pregnancy was brought about by the immunization or because I had lain down for so many months, we'll never know. We do plan to try for another baby, maybe in a year's time. It was a good thing we started young, wasn't it?

The Coagulation Effect of Certain Antibodies

As I mentioned at the beginning of this chapter, the inability to recognize your husband's tissue as foreign, and thereby to create the much-needed blocking factor, is not the only type of antibody disorder that is known to affect miscarriages. We also know that another immunologic problem may arise when the pregnant woman has what's called antiphospholipid antibodies, which promote blood clotting (coagulation). It has now been discovered that recurrent miscarriages may be due to these factors causing hypercoagulable states. This is a whole new area of research that may explain why many former miscarriages occurred.

The main difference between these two types of miscarriage is that the one involving antiphospholipid antibodies does not have a fixed pattern but often occurs later in the pregnancy than does a miscarriage involving the blocking factor. So, if you have miscarried in the first or second trimester and do not have uterine abnormalities, an incompetent cervix, or one of the more commonly looked for reasons, then special blood tests can be run to look for these coagulation-promoting antibodies.

The immunologic problem means that the mother's antibodies will attack some fatty substances on cell surfaces known as phospholipids. As the cells circulate, they produce an excess in clotting. The medical profession has been aware of the condition only in the past four to five years. Now, however, we do know that the excess clots may cause obstruction in small vessels or arteries, particularly those in the uterus in pregnancy, and in so doing they prevent the fetus from receiving its "food" of blood and oxygen. If this occurs, the fetus will die anytime up to the 20th week. It's as though a tap has been turned off.

The antiphospholipid antibodies that have been studied the most, and that have been identified as causes of recurrent pregnancy loss, are the anticardiolipin antibody and the lupus anticoagulant antibody. Other blood factors that may promote

coagulation and be a cause of miscarriages are also being studied. For example, an elevated platelet count may be a cause.
(Platelets are blood coagulation factors important in the normal
clotting process, but, if excessive, they can lead to the condition
known as thrombocytosis.) The effect of all these antibodies is
to inhibit the growth of the placenta and the transport of nutrients to the fetus. We do know, for example, that patients who
do *not* have the antibodies perform better in pregnancy than
those who do. So this form of investigation appears to be quite
important.

When the antibodies are found the treatment aims to diminish both the antibody level and the amount of clotting.
First, all other known causes of miscarriage must be eliminated.
Testing is done by taking a sample of your blood and sending
it to a center where this research is currently underway. Should
you test positive for any of these factors, there are different
forms of treatment available, depending on the different types
of antibodies.

Usually one baby aspirin a day is prescribed, which helps
to keep the blood "thin." This would be accompanied by daily
injections of an anticoagulant known as heparin. The medications should be taken once the pregnancy is diagnosed. If antibody levels are known to be very high, then baby aspirin may
even be taken from ovulation before the next pregnancy occurs. The medication should be continued until the end of the
pregnancy, although the use of baby aspirin is usually stopped
earlier, as it takes some time for its anticoagulating effect to
disappear. Heparin, by contrast, can be continued into the 9th
month as its effect is rapidly reversed by the body. Even going
into labor while still on the heparin should pose no problem.

How safe are these drugs in pregnancy? There is much
controversy over taking aspirin while pregnant because of the
alleged association with birth defects. However, there is not
the same link with baby aspirin, which is safe in pregnancy.
Heparin is known not to cross the placenta and is safely used

in pregnancy. Of course, while you are on these anticoagulants, you will be under close medical supervision. Your blood clotting will be tested regularly by a hematologist. The treatment should not put you at risk, in terms of everyday cuts or bruises. In fact, the effect on your blood coagulation will be hardly noticeable.

Heparin injections are usually given by the mother or her partner, after special training by the doctor or hematologist. The injections should not be painful, but they may cause a little bruising around the injection site. Sometimes, in place of heparin, a drug called prednisone, a form of cortisone, is used. This may be selected if, after blood testing, the heparin is not having the desired effect. But prednisone does have potential side effects, and heparin is usually preferred. You must rely, however, on your physician's advice. If you are on heparin or prednisone, you will need to take some extra calcium during your pregnancy.

This antibody theory and the theory involving rejection of your fetus constitute an entirely new area of investigation, and you must remember that the treatment protocols are not only new but still being researched. Side effects from the methods of treatment I have described are thought to be minimal. Although medication is not used in routine pregnancies, if you do suffer from recurrent miscarriage, you will probably agree that it is well worth it to take a small but calculated risk with medication in order to reach the all-important goal in your next pregnancy.

Here I will reintroduce Debbie, whom we met in chapter 1, where she talked about the grief mothers who miscarry bring with them as their lifelong burden. Now we can go further into her story, for Debbie is currently being treated with heparin and baby aspirin for the anticardiolipin antibody.

Debbie has a four-year-old daughter. But since that birth, she has suffered three miscarriages. Like those of several of the women in this book, Debbie's tale is one of frustration. But

with increasing knowledge, hopefully there will be fewer recurrent miscarriages.

"You Just Live Day by Day, and You Do It for the Baby."

I have one daughter, who was the result of my first pregnancy.
With my first miscarriage, I'd been close to 5 months pregnant, and
it was the last thing I'd expected to happen. I cried a lot at home,
but I dealt with my grief alone. I didn't want to upset my husband
or my daughter unnecessarily. When I told my doctor he suggested
that I get pregnant again. I thought everything would be fine the
next time.

I became pregnant again, but two months later I lost the
pregnancy. I began to panic. They say once is one of those things.
But twice? Next time, I intended to check everything out. So I
went to a fertility and miscarriage expert. I came to see the specialist with so much hope in my heart, because I was desperate. I would
honestly have done anything I was advised. My husband and I went
for many tests. Then I waited eighteen months because I was too
scared to risk getting pregnant again.

My next decision was to have my tubes tied. I felt that as I had
my daughter, I'd be safer leaving things as they were. Just as I made
the appointment for that operation, I changed my mind and decided I would give a pregnancy one last chance.

After further tests, it was shown that I had anti-cardiolipin
antibodies at a high level in my blood. I was put on baby aspirin
when next I conceived. At 8 weeks, when they could see the baby's
heartbeat on the scan, they started me on heparin. Now I have to
inject myself twice a day with the heparin, to keep my blood from
clotting. We were taught how to do it, but you should see my legs,
they're a real mess from the needles! I still take the baby aspirin
every day. But, as I see it, these drugs are the least of my problems.
To get a healthy baby at the end, if they told me to hang from the
ceiling four times a day, I would!

I go in for regular ultrasound scans when they check the
placenta. I feel much more reassured when I've been for a checkup.
Now I'm at the 15th week, and I'm praying hard. No matter how
confident I feel, still I'm scared. But every month it's another step

forward. You just live day by day, and you do it for the baby.

Of course I am worrying about the 22nd-week mark. The doctor watches everything. Every two weeks he checks my blood-clotting factors. I was on progesterone suppositories four times a day, and progesterone injections twice a week, until the 12th week, for extra security. I have been concerned about the effect of the heparin on the baby, but they tell me it doesn't go past the placenta to the baby. The one baby aspirin (which is a quarter of a regular one), also concerns me. I hate having to take drugs in pregnancy.

Now the doctor is talking about amniocentesis. And I'm scared. If, God forbid, something goes wrong, I don't know what I would do. I'd rather not take the risk of causing a miscarriage that way, having come this far.

I've never gotten over losing those pregnancies. Emotionally, it's all very hard. I can't pick my daughter up like I want to. I'm nervous if I'm hit in the stomach. I don't want sex. Since this pregnancy my husband and I haven't had intercourse. We're afraid to do anything we shouldn't. I used to go bowling for relaxation, but now I just go along with my husband to keep him company.

The doctors have told me I don't have to be so careful, that I can lead a normal life, because they feel it was placental clotting from that factor in my blood that was causing me to miscarry. But, until you have the baby in your arms, you can't erase the memory of those other miscarriages and feel content. Fortunately, I have been in touch with a woman from a pregnancy-loss support group who listens to me and reassures me that it is normal to have so many negative feelings and fears. Talking to her has also helped relieve the strain and tension between my husband and myself. It's helping us to communicate better.

6

Is It the Fault of Chromosomes?

HROMOSOMAL damage to the fetus? The thought preys heavily on the average woman's or man's mind when they lose a baby through a miscarriage. Most couples assume that the spontaneously lost baby was somehow malformed. Some people find they have recurrent dreams or nightmares that the baby was a kind of monster. Miscarriage is indeed commonly thought of as Nature's "quality control"; that she spontaneously self-destructs babies not perfect enough to be born.

There has been a misunderstanding here, at least for those unfortunate couples who have miscarried several times. Chromosomal damage is very likely to be the cause of a *first* miscarriage, one that happened before the 12th week. Indeed, up to 50 percent of first, early miscarriages are known to be caused by such problems. But a second or third miscarriage is less likely to have the same cause, because chromosomal deformity is *not* necessarily a recurring problem.

Genetic testing should be done to try to find the cause of

142

recurrent miscarriages. You should have the fetal tissue tested if it is possible to get it to a laboratory in a short time. That way, if the *karyotype*—the chromosomal alignment (see Figure 11)—is normal, you and your doctor can begin looking for other causes. To put it another way, if there was chromosomal damage, then your next pregnancy will probably be safe and secure, as a chromosomal abnormality is less likely to recur.

What Makes Chromosomal Problems Happen?

Advanced maternal age is the most well known cause. Why, is not fully understood. But as I mentioned in chapter 4, the eggs (ova) in you, the mother, may be showing the effects of growing older. There appears to be no link to your having taken birth control pills, and also no association with the sex of your fetus. It is, in fact, a myth that more baby boys, rather than girls, are lost due to miscarriage.

It is also possible that problems occur during the tenuous process of fertilization and the ensuing miraculous fusion of sperm and egg, which manage to combine to make one new human being.

When fertilization happens, at the time of ovulation, an egg is usually fertilized by one sperm in the fallopian tube. It all sounds so simple but, in fact, is very complicated because before conception the chromosomes of the egg and sperm cells must first divide *(meiosis),* so that each contains only 23 chromosomes (half the number for a human being). Then when they join, they will have the normal chromosome number, 46. If problems occur during this process, chromosomal abnormalities may result, which in turn may lead to a miscarriage.

But suppose your doctor has recommended you and your partner to attend genetic counseling, or the material from your miscarriage was sent to a genetics laboratory for chromosome testing. Just what information is your doctor looking for?

The Lives of Chromosomes and Genes

Our bodies are constructed of millions of cells, living, dying, changing all the time. Some cells live for a few months, others for years. The female egg cells, for example, can live for forty-five to fifty years. All these body cells contain chromosomes, which are long threadlike structures that operate in pairs and look something like two arms. The genes, containing the DNA code that imprints physical characteristics, such as the color of our hair and eyes, our blood type, and even our personalities, are in hundreds of miniscule dots on the chromosomes.

Unlike the genes, the chromosomes are distinguishable under the miscroscope. Back in the 1880s, it was discovered that these threadlike structures can absorb a special kind of dye and so become visible. (Their name derives from the Greek words, *chroma,* meaning color, and *soma,* meaning body.) Although we now use highly sophisticated techniques, the basis remains the same. The chromosomes are stained and investigated under magnification. The pairs are assessed for the right number, the proper structure, and the possibility of damage to individual ones.

Each of us has 46 chromosomes in every cell. Twenty-three of your chromosomes were inherited from your mother and the other 23 from your father, including one sex chromosome from each parent. If you inherited 1 x and 1 y chromosome, you became male; two x's and you became female. (See Figure 11.)

So each individual has 22 pairs, known as autosomes, plus its two sex chromosomes (the x's or y's), adding up to the requisite 46. As mentioned previously, during the process of *meiosis,* which occurs just before the moment of conception, each cell has only 22 autosomes plus 1 sex chromosome, so that when the sperm and egg lock sides, they will create one complete whole. When romantics write of falling in love, meaning you have found the "other half" to your whole, they are indeed quite right!

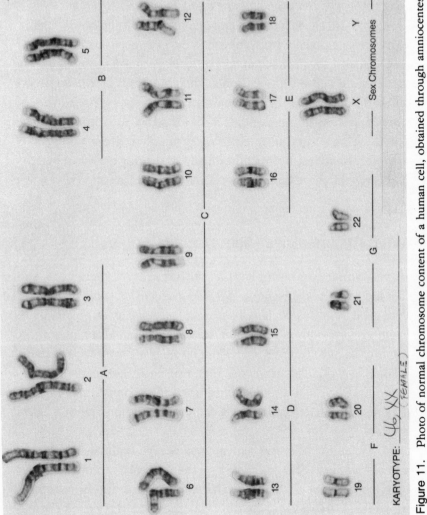

Figure 11. Photo of normal chromosome content of a human cell, obtained through amniocentesis.

145

Random selection decides which two cells, with particular genes attached to the chromosomes, will meet and mate, which is also why we are all so uniquely different. Genetic diseases therefore are set in motion from that moment of fertilization when the different genes meet and match.

The other important process of cell division is *mitosis,* which takes place within the twelve to twenty-four hours after the egg and sperm have met. This process marks the beginning of rampant cell multiplication as the conceptus begins to grow. At this stage some chromosomes can be lost or broken, or if there is an extra one present, it may lead to deformities. These kinds of abnormalities are usually miscarried early, and as I have emphasized before, they usually do not occur again, depending on the exact chromosomal configuration.

What Abnormalities Might Occur?

A very small number of couples with repeat miscarriages—and we are only talking of about 3 to 5 percent of those who have had recurrent miscarriages—may in fact have an abnormality in *their* chromosomes, in either partner, which does not affect their own lives but may affect the fetus. For example, an abnormality in your chromosomes may not be reflected in your appearance, but if it affects the number of chromosomes in your egg cell, then it could cause a problem when meiosis takes place.

A patient of mine had a certain rare malposition of her chromosomes. She was very upset to learn about this and needed a lot of reassurance that she was absolutely normal— not a freak. However, the only way they could try for a normal baby, unfortunately, was just to keep trying. They would possibly have to put up with repeated miscarriages until one conception managed to override the problem. Their chances of having a normal healthy baby, however, were good. The sad part is that in such a rare case, nothing can be done to prevent it or treat it. At this stage, there is no way we can alter the body's chromosomal makeup. Some day in the future, through work that is now being done with in vitro programs, genetic information will be extracted from a fertilized egg and preventive treatment given.

Similarly, another patient who was happily looking forward to her first baby discovered very sadly after amniocentesis that she, at the age of forty-three, had a polysomy 47XXX. We had to tell her that although such children are born looking normal, they are usually mentally abnormal. It was a terrible decision for her to make, but she decided to terminate the pregnancy. Again, she stands a good chance of a normal pregnancy the next time.

Translocation is a term you might come across in a discussion of chromosomes. With this condition, there is the correct number of chromosomes but the pieces are joined up incorrectly. You may have inherited this problem from one of your parents, but in your own conception it was balanced out. If a similar problem affects your partner, then it could be a cause of recurrent miscarriages for you as a couple. It is a rare condition, but one that should be tested for.

Most parents are very aware of a common birth defect, Down's syndrome, or mongolism, which is caused by an extra chromosome, usually no. 21, giving a count of 47, rather than 46. The condition is also known as trisomy 21. In the live-born baby, Down's syndrome results in the characteristic skin folds at the inner corner of the eyes, a large protruding tongue, small hands and fingers, as well as defects of the heart, eyes, ears, and various degrees of mental retardation. Many of these defective embryos, however, do miscarry in early pregnancy.

When Should You Go for Genetic Counseling?

If testing of a miscarriage specimen reveals abnormal chromosomes, your doctor will know to treat future pregnancies with extreme care and attention. You would be recommended to have an amniocentesis or chorionic villus sampling to ensure the absence of chromosomal disorders in the fetus.

If you are over thirty-five or your partner is over fifty-five, you should also consider genetics counseling because of the effect of aging.

Couples who are closely related—such as first cousins, second cousins, or uncle and niece—should also consider such counseling. First cousins have one-eighth of their genes in common. We all may have several defective recessive genes in our cells, which will cause a disorder only if one of these is able to make a pair with similar genes from a partner. For example, a man with a recessive gene for cystic fibrosis has only a 1 in 400 chance of marrying a carrier with a similar gene, when he is choosing a mate out of the general population. But, if he marries a first cousin, the odds escalate to 1 in 8. The risk of chromosomal abnormalities in their children increases from 1 in 1600 to 1 in 32 for each pregnancy.

Similarly, if you have previously given birth to a child with a congenital abnormality, even if the child was from a previous marriage, you should seek counseling to assess the risk.

What Happens at Genetic Counseling?

The counselor will ask you many, many questions about your families, going back as far as three generations. You will be asked medical details about any branch of either family—the number of miscarriages, stillbirths, children who died in infancy. Free forms, called Family Medical Records, can be obtained from the March of Dimes, so that you can begin working on them at home in preparation for the history taking.

If there are indications for further investigation, a blood test will be taken from you and your partner, which will be sent to a laboratory and examined for possible metabolic and chromosomal disorders. The results from these blood tests will take a few days. The delay is due to the time it takes your white blood cells to be drawn and then grown in the laboratory, in a petrie dish. When the cells begin to divide and multiply, as in the process described as mitosis, they will be compressed, and the chromosomes will be spread out, identified, and then matched into pairs.

If you are already pregnant, the geneticist can work with fetal cells found in the amniotic fluid and obtained by amniocentesis at about 16 weeks. Fetal cells for study can also be obtained by a new technique called chorionic villus sampling (CVS), which is done earlier in pregnancy (at about 9 weeks) than amniocentesis. This is an exciting and rapidly expanding new area of the science of reproduction, and one your doctor may make use of.

As I have mentioned earlier, some reassuring news for a couple who have experienced an early miscarriage would be to learn that its cause *was* chromosomal. You would then not need to take all the other tests to discover the possible causes of your miscarriage. Coupled with the fact that a major chromosomal problem in both parents is very rare, the news should make your next attempt at pregnancy a much less anxious time.

Infections as Causes of a Miscarriage

If you catch a bad cold, suffer from influenza ("flu") during pregnancy, or run a fever, it can be very frightening. If you then go on to miscarry, you're likely to think the virus was the cause of your loss, even though this is probably not so. In fact, we know quite a lot now about the role played by infections in recurrent miscarriages. Surprisingly, it is usually not the more obvious infections that are the most likely culprits. So your doctor may suggest running tests for infections, the names of which you have never previously heard and for which there may be no symptoms.

The good news is that many of these asymptomatic infections are treatable. Some have also been pinpointed as likely causes of *infertility*. Certain women have to take a course of antibiotics before becoming pregnant, and then they will remain on the antibiotics for at least some part of the pregnancy. It may also emerge one day that a blighted ovum or missed abortion has been the result of an infection.

What is this link between infections and miscarriage? It is possible that organisms could cause a miscarriage from as early as the time of conception. Organisms can attach themselves to the sperm and attack the egg on fertilization. Or, other organisms that are alive in either the male or female genital tracts might attack the fertilized egg either directly or via the sperm.

New knowledge and skills in treating these infections are yet other factors in today's management of recurrent miscarriages. There is much research underway about the link between infections and consequent infertility, miscarriage, and other obstetric problems such as premature labor. And more information is coming through all the time.

The exact relationship between a *specific* infection and a miscarriage is not always easy to prove. The infection, for example, that emerges in a test performed after a miscarriage might have occurred only following the death of this fetus. The vagina always contains certain organisms, and, in principle, any organism *could* cause a miscarriage providing it gained access to the uterine cavity. But, rest assured, organisms do not reach the uterus once pregnancy is established as the increased acidity of the vagina and the mucus plug in the cervix block their path. If your miscarriage was not obviously caused by other major problems, which have been discussed already, then it is important that you and your partner be tested for infections. If you had been undergoing problems with fertility, your partner's sperm and seminal fluid may have already been tested for infections when a sperm count was taken.

Now, let me run through a list of some infections that have been implicated in causing a miscarriage; some are historic, others are newer discoveries.

Syphilis

In France, some centuries ago, syphilis was called "the greatest aborter." Now rare, though its incidence is once again on the rise, it certainly does cause miscarriages. It can affect the fetus at any time during pregnancy, but especially in the beginning, at conception.

Mycoplasma

This organism causes a low-grade subclinical infection, that is, it does not cause any symptoms in the mother. You would show no signs of abnormality, as mycoplasma is also found in normal fertile women. The organism acts by causing chronic infection in the endometrium, or uterine lining. You might have noticed a fever following a miscarriage, which may be a telling sign. Mycoplasma is a cross between a bacteria and a virus, and lives in either the female or male genital tracts.

Mycoplasma was only identified as a cause of recurrent miscarriage in 1973, when studies identified a special kind of mycoplasma, called the T-strain, that showed up in many women who had undergone recurrent miscarriages.

To test for the organism, we take urine from both mother and father, plus a culture is taken from the woman's cervix. Between pregnancies, it can also be diagnosed by taking a biopsy of the inside of the uterine cavity (endometrial biopsy). If mycoplasma is identified, before you try for another pregnancy you and your partner would each be given a course of antibiotics, such as doxycycline (a form of tetracycline), for two weeks. If it is not discovered until you are already pregnant, similar treatment can be adopted, taking care to use an antibiotic that is safe in pregnancy.

Toxoplasmosis

Another infection that is likely to carry no symptoms, toxoplasmosis has been identified as a cause of sporadic or recurrent miscarriages. It is important to be able to make the diagnosis. Thankfully, sophisticated blood tests make that possible, but they are very specialized. However, it can also be detected by scraping the endometrial lining (endometrial biopsy). If the parasite is found in the biopsy, you would have to be treated for the infection.

You might have heard the rather "new wives' tale" that pregnant women should be careful around cats, covering their hands with rubber gloves when emptying a soiled cat litter tray. Toxoplasmosis is a parasitic infection transmitted by household pets and is known to lead to birth defects, miscarriage, premature labor, and stillbirth. Having said that, and alarming every cat owner in the nation, let me reassure you that its occurrence is very rare, about 1 in 8,000 pregnant women. There is no cause for alarm or need to move the cat out of the house during your pregnancy. *Just do not handle cat litter if you are pregnant.* Relegate the task to your partner. This is especially important if you do not have immunity to the organism. Most of us, however, are already immune to toxoplasmosis, having lived around household pets all our lives. Treatment is by pyrimethamine, sulfadiazine, and folic acid, and lasts for one month.

Exposure to cat feces is not the only way of being exposed to toxoplasmosis. The other methods of becoming infected are from eating raw meat such as steak tartare or raw fish such as sushi. So you should also avoid these foods in pregnancy. You will often be tested for immunity to toxoplasmosis as part of the prenatal blood-test package.

Chlamydia

One of the most common sexually transmitted organisms today is chlamydia. It is especially common among the young and sexually active and has been associated with impairment of fertility, so testing for chlamydia is now almost routine. Carriers of chlamydia are usually unaware of the infection because it causes no symptoms.

Present in the genital and urinary tracts of men and women, the organism does not invade the placenta or uterus, so we are not altogether sure of its role in causing a miscarriage. But it has been isolated from tissue following a miscarriage. To test for it, your doctor takes a sample of cervical mucus, much like a pap smear. Once diagnosed, both members of the couple are treated with a course of antibiotics.

Listeria

This is one of the organisms that until very recently was only indefinitely associated with miscarriages. However, the information on listeria has now changed. Recently, a team of microbiologists from Leeds, in England, showed that at least one-quarter of test samples of precooked chilled meats from supermarkets was contaminated with listeria, which has been shown to harm unborn, or even newborn, babies. The reason the listeria is present is thought to be because of shorter heating times for prepared foods, which do not guarantee the destruction of all bacteria. (Thorough cooking of meats, however, will destroy the bacteria.) Similarly, listeria has also been found in cheeses made from nonpasteurized milk. A case has been described of a pregnancy loss at 21 weeks from infected goat's-milk cheese.

It is now advised that pregnant women should be aware of the danger of eating *partially cooked* foods, including chicken, turkey, beef, and spare ribs, and they should also avoid soft cheeses or those made from unpasteurized milk.

Yeast or Monilia

This is a very common cause of vaginitis, which occurs with increased frequency in pregnancy because of an elevated sugar content in the vaginal cells and the high acidity of the vagina itself. *Monilia* has been associated with causing a miscarriage but only when an intrauterine device (IUD) has been in place. The IUD may itself be the cause of miscarrying the pregnancy. It probably is *not* important as a cause of miscarriage. But, if *Monilia* is present in pregnancy, it should be treated, because it causes discomfort and may also infect the baby as it passes through the vagina. It can cause an episiotomy to heal poorly. Safe treatment with nystatin is available in pregnancy.

Malaria

In parts of the world where malaria is endemic, it can cause a miscarriage, probably because of the associated high fever or circulatory disturbance in the placenta. But this is not usually a cause for concern unless you have been traveling in parts of the world where malaria is a danger. If you are in early pregnancy, it would be advisable to avoid such areas.

Many other bacteria have been given as causes of miscarriages. In theory, they travel through the mother's bloodstream and can reach the fetus across the placenta, but generally they are too large to cross the placental barrier. Much still needs to be learned about the association between infection and miscarriage.

Infections Associated with Certain Procedures

Insertion of the Cervical Stitch (Shirodkar)

The later a stitch is inserted into the cervix, say after 18 weeks, the greater the chance of infection occuring there, which, in turn, may mean the membranes will become infected, thus enabling the fetus to be affected or the membranes to rupture. We are not sure why there is greater protection if the stitch is placed earlier. Antibiotics are often given following the procedure as a precaution. This is also one reason why the stitch should be removed about two weeks before you expect to go into labor, as it will give your body time to destroy any cervical infection associated with the stitch and will prevent the uterus from becoming infected after delivery.

IUD in Place

If your pregnancy is diagnosed while you have an intra-uterine device (IUD) still in place, infection may be a significant problem, as the IUD acts as a foreign body in the uterus promoting infection. There is a greater risk of infection if the strings of the device are protruding into the vagina, as they may act as a track for infection to follow into the uterus. The doctor usually removes the device if the strings are visible. So, if pregnancy occurs with an IUD in place, there is an increased risk of miscarriage.

Campylobacter

An organism that causes gastroenteritis has also been implicated in causing miscarriages. We do not understand how it leads to miscarriage.

Intercourse

Apart from the prostaglandins in semen, which have been mentioned as a potential cause of difficulties if you have previously miscarried (as the prostaglandins can make the uterus contract as if you were in premature labor), there is another reason to be cautious about intercourse if miscarriage is a problem. Bacteria can be carried on the sperm, and, if in the second trimester your cervix is short or already a little bit open, the bacteria might enter the uterus and infect the fetus. The bacteria so introduced could lead to infection of the membranes and the danger of their rupture, or they may bring about increased uterine contractions. These risks do not apply in normal pregnancy, where intercourse is *not* forbidden.

Anal intercourse should be avoided, if vaginal intercourse is prohibited.

Rely on your doctor's advice regarding intercourse in high-risk pregnancy situations. The use of a condom may be advised in some circumstances.

Viruses

As is the case with bacteria, the exact roles of different viruses in causing miscarriages is unknown. There are several difficulties in assessing the role of viruses. Firstly, it is difficult and complicated to isolate a virus from miscarried tissue. Also viral disease is common in and out of pregnancy—even the common cold has been implicated in sporadic miscarriages. Yet there are certain viruses that are known to be dangerous in pregnancy.

German Measles (Rubella)

This virus crosses the placenta and infects both the placenta and fetal tissue, causing either congenital abnormalities or a spontaneous miscarriage. We do not know how often miscarriages are caused by rubella, as most reports focus on the abnormalities found at the birth if the pregnancy continues.

Any woman who contracts German measles in the early weeks of pregnancy would be *seriously* advised against continuing her pregnancy, as, in early pregnancy, there is an 85 percent chance that rubella could cause some major abnormality such as blindness, heart disease, or limb defects. While it is preventable by vaccination before you are pregnant, you cannot be vaccinated against rubella once pregnant. Although the virus in the vaccination is weak it is nevertheless alive and could damage the fetus. You can have a blood test done before you get pregnant to see if you need to be immunized against the disease.

Genital Herpes

This virus may cause a miscarriage if you have the *initial* attack in early pregnancy—during the first 20 weeks. It is believed that the virus may cross the placenta and infect the embryo or fetus. Usually, the first attack of herpes is more severe than recurring attacks, and it is accompanied by a high fever. It is not known for certain whether the fever or the herpes virus actually causes the miscarriage.

Remember, if you have already had an attack of herpes and become pregnant, the recurring attacks are not believed to cause a miscarriage or any fetal abnormalities. So do not be concerned if you or your husband have a history of herpes. A recurring attack will only be significant in pregnancy if it causes a lesion, or *ulcer,* on the cervix, vagina, or the labia, which is still present when you go into labor. In that case, you would require a delivery by C-section to avoid the baby's coming into contact with the virus (in the ulcer). The drug effective against herpes, acyclovir, is not safe to use during pregnancy.

Other Viruses

The AIDS (acquired immunodeficiency syndrome) virus itself does not cause a miscarriage but could be associated with general maternal illness, which may do it. *Cytomegalovirus* was once thought to be a cause of miscarriages, although no known link has yet been discovered. *Mumps, measles, Hepatitis A* and *B,* and *Parvovirus* may also have links with miscarriage. So, as you can gather from the above, the exact role of some viruses in causing miscarriages is uncertain given our current knowledge.

Can You Be Vaccinated During Pregnancy?

Is it safe for the fetus? is the question asked by so many women who require vaccination *during* pregnancy. This is one of those complex issues that needs to be talked through seriously with your doctor; the pros and cons will have to be weighed by you and your partner before making a decision. As a general rule, it is thought that the fetus is more endangered by *living vaccines,* for example, those against rabies, yellow fever, polio, smallpox, mumps, measles, and German measles, than by inactivated vaccines, such as those for whooping cough, typhoid, cholera, influenza, and polio. Tetanus toxoid vaccine, given as a booster against a possible tetanus risk, is considered safe.

The following story, told by Maureen, brings together much of the information we have been dealing with in this chapter and in earlier sections of the book. Her connection with the infection theme goes back to the link with mycoplasma and infertility. The treatment worked for Maureen and her husband. But then she suffered three miscarriages. She has used progesterone therapy and ultimately also immunization therapy.

"We Hardly Dared to Let Ourselves Feel Happy"

My husband has a child of eleven from a previous marriage. It was the second marriage for both of us, but I'd never tried to have a baby before meeting him. Five years ago when we married, we decided to try to begin a family immediately. I was thirty-three and felt I was ready to become a mother. Well, I didn't get pregnant that year. It was awful for me because I knew my husband was fertile, so I felt it must all be my fault. My periods had started late and had always been irregular, so deep down I felt I might not be able to have a child. Previously, I'd been to see a top gynecologist, and he suggested I have a hysterogram to take a look inside. That was a very painful and uncomfortable experience. One of my tubes seemed to be blocked, and I have a T-shaped uterus. I was warned then I'd have a hard time holding a pregnancy.

Anyway, we finally went to see an infertility specialist. By the time the appointment actually came through, two years had already passed by with no conception.

The specialist said I was relatively young to be panicking about being infertile, but he ran a lot of tests and it turned out I had an infection called mycoplasma—for which there are no symptoms, but which can lead to infertility. I took antibiotics for a period of two months, and then I became pregnant! We were so excited. But after three months, I began bleeding and lost the pregnancy.

I was so upset that we waited three months before going back to see the specialist. We were recommended for genetics counseling. But, genetically, it seemed we were fine. The specialist wanted me to have a whole series of tests, rather than risk having another miscarriage. But, at the time, I felt a lot of people have one miscarriage, so I turned the idea down. Again he discovered I had mycoplasma, and once again it was cleared up with antibiotics, and I became pregnant.

I was put on progesterone suppositories and was going for weekly blood tests to check progesterone levels. But, by the 8th or 9th week, I started to bleed. When I went in for a sonogram, we saw there was no heartbeat. I had to have a D & C. By now, I'd had two miscarriages, and I was beginning to be very upset. We turned to a miscarriage specialist, and this time when he offered to run special tests to find out why I kept losing the pregnancies, I was ready to do more.

Mycoplasma was treated once more, and not long afterward I became pregnant again. I was back on progesterone, with blood tests every week. But I think I felt doomed. We hardly dared to let ourselves feel happy. My husband and I drive to work together.

As the days passed we ticked them off. And when we passed the stage where I had bled previously, we felt great relief.

But, just before the 10th week, when I went in for a sonogram, again there was no heartbeat. He asked for a second opinion, but it was confirmed. After this miscarriage, we went for immunization testing. By now I was thirty-six years old, and I was getting very scared. The results came back that we were eligible, but I didn't know what it meant. Besides, I'd decided I didn't want to get pregnant anymore. I couldn't deal with the ups and downs, and it no longer felt a positive thing to be doing. But my husband was determined and said let's try one more time.

We went back to the specialist and were advised to go for the immunological treatment. I needed to be immunized with my husband's blood, which was then done.

But, before I could get pregnant, again mycoplasma had to be treated. For the first time ever, I conceived by accident—we weren't even trying at that time! It was quite a surprise as I'd had an infertility problem. But it made me feel good, as though fate was on our side. And, from the beginning things felt different. I used to go to dancing school after work. I loved the classes and always had a big debate with myself whether I should give up when I was pregnant. But I felt so *healthy* this time, and I kept up one class, which was a very slow and gentle stretch exercise class.

Because I was so nervous and couldn't bear a replay of the same old story, I phoned up a laboratory myself and made an appointment for a sonogram. I was sitting there on pins and needles. Would there be a heartbeat or not? Finally the sonographer said, "There it is." My husband was waiting in the doorway, and we both had tears in our eyes.

A week later we went to my doctor; he advised me to go home and rest for at least the next two weeks. Those two weeks I really rested, then I got up a little more, and, after five weeks, I returned to work.

In fact, the only problem I had during the pregnancy was very bad hemorrhoids. Most of the time I felt in terrific condition. In the end, I went into labor, and there I was holding my little girl. When I think back, I know there was a point I would have accepted not having a baby at all. Now I just feel really lucky. Without all that persevering and help from doctors, I'd never have known how wonderful it can be. We'll always wonder if it was the treating of the mycoplasma which was the main help, or the immunization treatment. Maybe this was just the lucky one. A friend says girls are stronger. It doesn't matter in the end; for me a baby is certainly a very precious thing.

7

... Or a Problem You May Never Have Thought Of?

Sometimes the most obvious cause of a miscarriage will be completely overlooked by the grieving couple. Where the woman may be guiltily focusing on the fact she went shopping, cleaned the house, helped move furniture, or did that exercise class she feared was not suitable, there may be a simpler answer. At the same time, her partner may be silently worrying over his alcohol consumption, cigarette smoking, or failure to help her carry the groceries that day before she lost the baby.

Because these kinds of fears, worries, and guilt inducers are all too common for both men and women who have lost a pregnancy through miscarriage, in this chapter I bring together the last few *known* causes of miscarriage, and show how the suspected causes above are now known not to be culprits.

Advanced Maternal Age

This is an obvious cause but one often overlooked by those trying to begin a family around the age of forty. As a woman passes the age of thirty-five, her chances of miscarrying increase. The reasons are similar to those I have discussed before; they are usually based on chromosomal problems. Abnormalities of the ovum may be involved, for example, or chromosomal problems that would have led to a fetus having trisomy 21 (Down's syndrome), which usually causes miscarriage early in pregnancy (see table, p. 164).

Whether older women, in fact, miscarry more often or whether they *report* more miscarriages is a debatable point. A younger woman may attribute heavy bleeding one month to a late period, particularly if she did not want to be pregnant. Whereas an older woman, if she has previously been pregnant and has a living child, will more readily recognize the symptoms of pregnancy; she will usually have a strong commitment to being pregnant and will therefore rush to report a miscarriage to her doctor.

There are also surprising statistics for an increased miscarriage rate in very young mothers, under the age of eighteen. Why this is so is not known. It could be a reflection of socioeconomic factors; such young women undergoing pregnancy are more likely to have come from lower socioeconomic classes, with poorer nutrition and general standards of health care. Or, it could be a reflection of the likelihood of first pregnancies to miscarry more frequently.

Paternal Age

The father's advancing age also has an effect on the baby's health and welfare. There is an increased risk of chromosomal abnormalities of the sperm as a man ages, which may have the same influence on the rate of miscarriage as does the age of a

Risk of having a liveborn child with Down's Syndrome by one year maternal age intervals from ages 20–49 years.*

Maternal Age	Risk of Down's Syndrome
20	1/1923
21	1/1695
22	1/1538
23	1/1408
24	1/1299
25	1/1205
26	1/1124
27	1/1053
28	1/990
29	1/935
30	1/885
31	1/826
32	1/725
33	1/592
34	1/465
35	1/365
36	1/287
37	1/225
38	1/177
39	1/139
40	1/90
41	1/85
42	1/67
43	1/53
44	1/41
45	1/32
46	1/25
47	1/20
48	1/16
49	1/12

As you can see from the table, the risk of having a Down's syndrome baby changes appreciably from age 37. Many medical centers will now perform amniocentesis on women who are 35 years or over.

Data of Hook and Chambers (1977), from the World Symposium of Perinatal Medicine, San Francisco, 1981.

woman over thirty-five. If the father is over fifty-five, the risk of miscarriage is particularly significant, and amniocentesis is recommended, whether the mother is over thirty-five or not, particularly because of the risk of Down's syndrome.

Fathers of advanced age may be at risk for new mutations of genes in their sperm.

Paternal Disorders

Semen quality used to be thought of as a reason for a woman to miscarry. But now there seems to be no evidence that a low sperm count has any significant effect. However, polyspermy— where too many sperm are in the seminal fluid (more than 250 million sperm in every milliliter of seminal fluid)—has been questioned as a cause of miscarriage. So far there is no strong evidence for this association.

The immunological argument has also been brought in, however, to add weight to the discussion of sperm influencing miscarriages. Some women, we now know, have antibodies to their husband's sperm in their blood. After conception, the embryo, which could contain the same antigens as the father's sperm, may be rejected by the mother due to the sperm antibodies in her blood. There is no strong evidence to support this theory, but we can test for sperm antibodies in the mother's blood.

Severe Morning Sickness

It would be unusual for the nausea and vomiting of early pregnancy to cause a miscarriage. Even severe disturbances of metabolism, caused by frequent vomiting in pregnancy, which can disturb the body's normal mineral and electrolyte balance, do not cause a miscarriage.

However, there are maternal diseases, like lupus, that we know can lead to miscarriages.

Systemic Lupus Erythematosus (SLE)

SLE is a disturbance of the immune system, which means the patients form antibodies against their *own* tissues. It is a much more common disorder in women than in men, and unfortunately it affects women particularly in their childbearing years. SLE is one illness which has been associated with an increased rate of miscarriage in part because there is an increased incidence of anti-phospholipid antibodies. You should be tested for SLE if your doctor is running tests for the causes of a miscarriage; all that is needed is a blood sample, which is tested for antibodies to DNA.

We are not sure why this kind of miscarriage occurs, but antibodies are a probable cause. Fortunately, modern medical treatment often using steroids, such as prednisone, is effective in keeping SLE under control and has allowed patients with this disease to carry pregnancies to term.

Usually women with SLE are already aware of the condition, and their doctors treat such pregnancies with due care and caution. Without treatment the miscarriage rate would be as high as 30 percent. Usually the loss occurs between the 2nd and 3rd month of the pregnancy in untreated cases.

Heart Disease

If you were born with certain types of congenital heart disease, you may be more likely to miscarry, because the fetus may not receive adequate oxygen from your circulation. This does not apply to patients with heart murmurs or to patients diagnosed as having a mitral valve prolapse (MVP), which is a relatively benign condition increasingly diagnosed in otherwise healthy young women.

Thyroid Disorders

Although there is still no firm evidence that thyroid disorders are associated with recurrent miscarriage, historically women with underactive thyroid (hypothyroid) have been seen to be at greater risk. Many research studies have tried to prove a definite link, but so far without success. However, so strong is the association in many people's minds, that often a small dose of synthetic thyroid (in itself not harmful to pregnancy) is sometimes given to a recurrent miscarrier in the hope that it might be of some help. At present, however, neither underactive nor overactive (hyperactive) thyroid has been conclusively proved as a cause of miscarriage. You might have a blood sample taken, nevertheless, which would be sent to the laboratory to test for thyroid disorders. And, if your doctor does recommend thyroid medication, there is no cause for concern about fetal defects.

Diabetes Mellitus

Some people strongly believe that diabetes is associated with an increased risk of miscarriage. However, this has not been conclusively demonstrated. Just as with SLE (systemic lupus erythematosus), if the illness is controlled the miscarriage rate doesn't go up. Most of the studies reporting such a link were from the 1960s, when diabetes control was not as efficient as it is today.

There is definitely no increase in miscarriages in *gestational* diabetes, that is, in patients who have diabetes only when pregnant (which has resulted from pregnancy hormones interfering with the action of insulin). But some studies have shown slightly increased miscarriage rates in *frank* diabetes, that is, in insulin-treated diabetics who become pregnant. However, even then it is avoidable, and there is no real difference between this group and nondiabetic women who become pregnant. A glucose-tolerance test, in which glucose is given as a drink and the blood is tested for up to three hours after the drink, is therefore not necessary as part of a routine workup in recurrent miscarriage. Rates of miscarriage seem only to increase in *uncontrolled* diabetes.

Endometriosis

This is a common disorder in women and a cause of infertility. Some studies also suggest that it may cause miscarriages, though the exact basis for this is not understood. The miscarriage rate was thought to be lower in women who have the endometriosis treated, either medically or surgically. The role of this disease as a cause of miscarriage is uncertain.

Nutrition

The role of nutrition in medicine is becoming more important than ever. There is no certain evidence that a dietary lack of any single nutrient is a significant cause of a miscarriage. At the present time, there is no strong evidence linking even malnutrition to an increased rate of miscarriages. But pregnancy is certainly no time to be dieting, and those women in poorer circumstances, without access to fresh foods, fruits, and vegetables, may well run a higher risk of miscarriage.

Women often worry that their nausea, vomiting, or lack of appetite, in the first trimester (12 weeks) of pregnancy, may cause a miscarriage. They feel their nutritional levels are so poor that the baby is being starved. In fact, even when the vomiting has reached extreme proportions, requiring hospitalization (known medically as *hyperemesis gravidarum*), there is still no increase in the rate of miscarriage.

Ironically, it is often true that the *more* nauseated you are in early pregnancy, the less chance you will have of miscarrying. Those aggravating symptoms of nausea and the extreme fatigue in the first trimester may be indications that the hormone levels required by the pregnancy are adequate.

Migraine

Migraine was once given as a cause of miscarriages, but this is not true. The association probably came about because of ergotamine compounds, which were given as a treatment for migraine during early pregnancy and which probably caused the pregnancy losses. This method of treatment must not be given in pregnancy. Migraine in itself is not a cause of miscarriages.

Coagulation Disorders

Von Willebrand's disease is a blood disorder—the lack of a factor that helps clot the blood. Some studies have indicated that patients with this disease miscarry recurrently. But this is not necessarily true, because other women with the disorder have had several successful pregnancies. If you have a family history of this or other bleeding problems, you should be tested before you get pregnant. If diagnosed, the disorder can be treated.

Further, patients who lack certain factors in the blood necessary for normal blood clotting control may have an increased chance of miscarrying. When blood coagulation occurs, it goes through certain steps. Measurement for these factors is done as part of a routine workup in unexplained miscarriages.

ABO Blood Group Compatibility

Studies about the role of ABO blood group incompatibility between the parents, as a possible cause of either infertility or recurrent miscarriage, have been inconclusive. But there is a strong suggestion that incompatibility of the major blood groups, such as the ABO, does play a role.

So it appears that if the parents do not share the same ABO grouping, and if the fetus is of a different ABO type from its mother, then there is an increased risk of losing the pregnancy. The only preventive way to determine this would be to measure the ABO type of a miscarriage specimen. If the mother and the specimen were both the same type, one could say this was *not* a cause of miscarriage. Research is needed in this area. At the moment a routine determination of the specimen's blood group is not done.

There is a rare blood group system, called the P system, and the presence of anti-P antibodies in a mother's blood has been given as a cause of miscarriage. How it causes miscarriages is not known. It occurs if the father has the P system in his blood. Fortunately it is very rare and is not routinely tested for.

Liver Disease

This is not a cause of recurrent miscarriage, though a rare condition called Wilson's disease, a disturbance of copper metabolism, has been associated with pregnancy loss. It can be tested by measuring a substance called caeruloplasmin in the mother's blood and can be successfully treated.

Stress and Anxiety

Psychological factors that might cause a miscarriage are very different from the psychological effects of having had a miscarriage (which you will read more about in chapter 8). Work was carried out in the 1950s and 1960s in New York and Nova Scotia on psychological factors in women who had miscarried repeatedly. Although the two groups of reseachers found slightly different characteristics, it was detemined that those miscarriage-prone women were immature and dependent with dominant mothers. Additionally these women showed poor emotional control and a tendency to guilt feelings. Reseachers felt that these personality traits may have caused miscarriages. However, it is now felt that these traits may be a result of having had the miscarriage, which is now known to be emotionally traumatic.

It is important to determine whether stress, as so many parents believe, can cause a miscarriage. A study to determine the effects of stress on the course of a pregnancy is almost impossible to carry out, as it would entail isolating a woman in a room and measuring her stress hormone levels throughout the entire pregnancy. However, it has already been shown that stress and grief can effect immunologic fuctioning, which may be one mechanism through which miscarriages are caused.

It has been suggested, too, that emotional factors may interfere with the pregnancy implanting in the uterus. Stress may also act on the body's hormones. Could adrenalin and other stress hormones trigger a miscarriage? These are very commonly asked questions. Even though all the evidence is not in yet, relieving stress and anxiety is very important in pregnancy. There are reported studies that have shown the beneficial effects of psychological support on women who have undergone several miscarriages. Tender love and care (T.L.C.) and, of course, good medical care may contribute to a high success rate in pregnancies. The consensus now is that the psychological factor is *not* a cause of miscarriage. But in general, stress is now seen as an important factor in the field of medicine and as something to be kept under control wherever possible. It is known that stress has an effect on immune system disorders that can lead to all sorts of medical illnesses. There is certain to be more research emerging in this area.

Nevertheless, the type of care you receive is extremely important. Reassurance, constant support with medical backup, and occasional ultrasound scans from the 7th to the 8th week to see the fetal heartbeat—all help the mother believe that her pregnancy is healthy and that she can achieve her goal. I believe that a firm, but advised, positive attitude can be tremendously helpful.

Physical Trauma

Although many women tend to relate their miscarriages to some event such as heavy lifting, a fall, or even a blow to the abdomen, physical trauma is, in fact, an unlikely cause of miscarriage. As we read previously in Rachel's story, even an automobile accident in late pregnancy did not cause her to miscarry.

And we have all heard tales of young women desperately wishing *not* to be pregnant, going to extremes of jumping from high walls or falling down, and still failing to cause a miscarriage.

Early in pregnancy, the bony pelvis shields the uterus from the impact of a blow. Everyday trauma, such as a pelvic examination or sexual intercourse, will not *cause* a miscarriage. Falls, slips, or inadvertent blows to the abdomen are not usually a danger. Neither is your toddler's jumping up and down on your tummy. The loss of the pregnancy will only ensue if the miscarriage was inevitable anyway. Many women worry about having a pelvic examination if they are bleeding in early pregnancy. But it is safe and, besides giving the doctor useful information, will not cause a miscarriage.

Physical trauma could affect your pregnancy if it is a penetrating injury such as a stab or bullet wound, which of course would harm you and the fetus.

Prior Induced Abortion (Termination)

Doctors used to believe that vaginal termination of pregnancy carried an increased risk of miscarriage in subsequent pregnancies. But this is not so. Before abortion became legal, some terminations were carried out late in the pregnancy, as there were no medical resources. If the cervix was forcibly dilated, an incompetent cervix could be the result (see chapter 4).

Now with early pregnancy diagnosis and the ability to terminate earlier, cervical damage should not be as great a problem. There are also ways of avoiding cervical trauma during procedures. Your doctor may use prostaglandins or laminaria the night before the abortion to dilate the cervix slowly and thus avoid the use of mechanical dilators.

Of course, it is a good idea to limit the number of induced abortions. If you have undergone a previous termination of pregnancy, do not be shy about letting your doctor know—just in case cervical incompetence does prove to be a problem. At least he can be aware of the potential for such a problem.

Exercise and Sporting Activities

Only certain women should be discouraged from exercising vigorously during pregnancy: those who have suffered more than one miscarriage, those who have had any bleeding or cramping in early pregnancy, and those who have been recommended to take bed rest.

Exercise, other than moderate walking and daily activities, like light running for the bus, should then be avoided. If your doctor has recommended bed rest, avoid any unnecessary exercise. Whatever weight you will gain in pregnancy will just have to be worked off vigorously once you have had your baby. You may be able to resume exercising later, once your doctor has advised more normal activities. Exercise and sporting activities, in themselves, will not cause a miscarriage. Aerobics, twisting exercises, jogging, bicycling, and certainly swimming are all safe in normal pregnancies.

Swimming, long known to be one of the safest forms of exercise, comes in for a lot of suspicion during pregnancy. Many women have heard stories that the water might enter the vagina and so adversely affect the fetus. There is no danger of water getting into the vagina, and by implication the uterus, neither will it affect your bloodstream. So, unless you have been warned against it, and if you enjoy swimming, it is an excellent form of exercise for the pregnant woman.

Competitive sports such as squash and raquetball should be avoided—unless you play them regularly—as the sudden bursts of excess energy could cause a physical injury. A prolonged rise in body temperature can have a harmful effect on the developing fetus. So avoid more than thirty minutes of intense exercise, as this may raise the core temperature of your body. Similarly, prolonged exposure to heat, such as that from a sauna or whirlpool bath, should be avoided or kept to just a few minutes. Jogging is fine but not at marathon levels.

Needless to say, certain sports that carry a risk of physical danger should be avoided: Horseback riding and mountaineering could lead to falls, skiing has its known dangers, and hang gliding is definitely out.

Burn Injuries

The trauma from something as frightening as receiving severe burns will not necessarily lead to miscarriage, unless the damage to your body was extensive and life threatening, causing major damage. Minor burns do not cause miscarriages and are not dangerous in pregnancy.

The Risks of Medical Devices and Procedures Before and During Pregnancy

Contraceptive Devices

Many women worry about their use of contraceptive methods prior to becoming pregnant, particularly if there was no real gap between stopping the contraception and conceiving.

If you conceived during the first cycle after you stopped taking birth control pills, you run no greater risk of miscarriage than you would normally. It is harmful to be taking the pill only while you are pregnant.

However, if an intrauterine device (IUD) is in place when you conceive, then you do run an increased risk of having a miscarriage. The IUD has a higher failure rate than the pill— about 2 out of 100 women using it in one year (versus 7/10 out of 100 women using the pill for a year). If you do become pregnant with an IUD in place, your risk factor increases to 25 out of 100 of having a miscarriage. You will have to discuss with your doctor whether you should have the IUD removed or terminate this pregnancy.

As far as is known, the diaphragm and contraceptive sponge, jelly, gel, and foam have no effect on rates of miscarriage. Spermicides were once implicated in causing chromosome abnormalities, but this research has not been reproduced nor shown to be true.

Ovulation-Inducing Agents

If you have been taking ovulation-inducing agents such as clomiphene citrate (can be Clomid or Serophene) or human menopausal gonadotrophins (can be Pergonal), the most commonly used of these fertility drugs, the risk of a miscarriage increases. It is generally agreed, however, that women with fertility problems have an increased risk of miscarriage to begin with. If you fall into this category, your doctor will follow you very closely in the early stages of pregnancy, by monitoring your hormone levels. Once again, this means that many more early miscarriages are detected and reported. We are not, therefore, sure whether the increased rate reflects a *real* change in the figures, or whether simply more data are recorded.

Clomiphene, an antiestrogen chemical (not a hormone), has a miscarriage rate of just under 20 percent, and Pergonal has a miscarriage rate of just over 20 percent. No one knows exactly why this is, and these figures, of course, cannot be exact. If your prolactin level is high, you might be given a drug called bromocriptine to lower it. The miscarriage rate for this drug is just over 10 percent.

The cause of these miscarriages, however, may be an inadequate corpus luteum function (described in chapter 3, page 68). Pregnancies of women who have previously been infertile, as we have seen, are often supported by progesterone suppositories in the first trimester.

Amniocentesis or Chorionic Villus Sampling (CVS)

Amniocentesis is the name given to the extraction of amniotic fluid for chromosomal analysis, or genetics testing on the baby. This is usually performed at around 16 weeks of pregnancy, when there is sufficient amniotic fluid to make its removal safe. An ultrasound is done first to locate the fetus, placenta, and pool of fluid. The doctor inserts a hollow needle through the woman's abdominal wall, and the amniotic fluid is drawn up through the needle into the vial. You will have to wait about seven to ten days (it used to be four to five weeks) for the results, while the cells are grown and the chromosomes are investigated.

It can be alarming for the pregnant woman, already entering her fifth month, to watch the giant needle invading her abdomen and to worry about whether this will cause a miscarriage. Surprisingly, the procedure is not at all painful. Amniocentesis does carry a small further risk of miscarriage, but this has lessened over the years as doctors become more and more skilled in the procedure. The risk factor can run from 1 in 200, to 1 in 400, with a doctor who performs amnios frequently.

Chorionic villus sampling (CVS) is a new technique, still considered at the research stage, whereby a small sample of chorionic (placental) tissue is taken at about the 9th or 10th week of pregnancy, by inserting a tube through the cervix or sometimes through the abdomen. Results are available within seven to ten days. The advantage of CVS is that it can be performed earlier in pregnancy, so that if a serious chromosomal defect is discovered, a termination could be performed earlier.

The disadvantage of CVS is that it still carries a higher risk of miscarriage than amniocentesis. Currently the risk is given as 1 in 100. Further, with CVS, confusion may arise if there is a mixture of chromosome karyotypes in the rapidly growing placental cells.

Since both procedures carry a risk of miscarriage, women who have already suffered several pregnancy losses may find that putting this pregnancy at further risk is untenable. You and your partner will have to debate with each other and with your doctor the value of the test and its side effects very carefully. If you do have a history of recurrent miscarriage, amniocentesis is probably the safer procedure. It also offers alpha-fetoprotein (AFP) sampling from the fluid at the same time. With CVS, the AFP sample would have to be done later. (However, the AFP test has a high incidence of false positives and needs to be repeated often, which may lead to unnecessary anxiety.)

As you will have read in some of the stories in this book, many women have had to go through this difficult decision process. Very often, despite their reluctance to terminate a pregnancy after years of struggling to save one, they do have the chromosomal testing because of their fear of not being able ever to have a normal healthy child.

DES Exposure

A synthetic estrogen, diethylstilbestrol, or DES, started to be used on pregnant women in 1948. Because it could control bleeding, it was thought to be useful in certain pregnancy disorders such as threatened miscarriage and premature labor. Its use was discontinued in 1971, so that anyone born afterward could not have been exposed to its side effects. The first reports of its harmful effects on the female offspring of its users were abnormal changes in the vagina, even cancer of the vagina.

However, subsequent reports also noted that abnormalities of the uterus occurred in the offspring of the mothers who had used DES. Particularly, the uterine cavity of a DES daughter could be reduced in size, underdeveloped, or misshapen, typically as a T-shaped uterus. Sometimes adhesions were found inside the uterine cavity. Also the cervix could be incompetent, or weak. Tubal (ectopic) pregnancies and premature labor are also more common after DES exposure.

These conditions all increased the risk of miscarriage, and the evidence was borne out in studies showing that DES daughters had a higher miscarriage rate than other women. Fortunately, this is a self-limiting illness because DES is no longer used in pregnancy. There are ways to treat all these conditions, as described in chapter 4. Where there is an incompetent cervix, for example, a stitch will help save the pregnancy.

If you have had a miscarriage and know your mother took DES, you should have a hysterosalpingogram to look for abnormalities in the uterus or cervix. Further, if your obstetrician knows that you are a DES daughter, he will watch your pregnancies carefully, and the state of your cervix will be frequently checked to see if it is shortening or opening too early.

Surgery During Pregnancy

Whether surgery during pregnancy will *cause* a miscarriage is not known for certain. If surgery must be performed, the earlier in the pregnancy the better, particularly during the first trimester. Pelvic surgery, such as removal of an ovarian cyst or an appendix, especially may be a culprit. However, if surgery cannot be avoided, a special anesthesia can be given so the fetus is well oxygenated. Anesthetic agents that cause fetal abnormalities in the first trimester of pregnancy must be avoided. In midtrimester surgery, drugs such as progesterone or ritodrine (uterine relaxants) may be given for the first two weeks or so following the procedure.

It is not definite as to whether surgery causes any harm during pregnancy, but any elective surgery (that can be postponed) should be avoided until after the baby's born. Or, if it is necessary to remove a gall bladder, for instance, because of gall stones, surgery could be performed before you become pregnant.

Surgery to remove fibroids should not be done during pregnancy unless the fibroid is attached to the surface of the uterus and can safely be removed.

Acute appendicitis is very difficult to diagnose in pregnancy, because the pain may not be felt in the typical area due to the altered position of the appendix.

In Vitro Fertilization

We discussed in vitro fertilization earlier, and mentioned that the procedure does carry an increased risk of miscarriage in the ensuing pregnancy. The risk factor used to be given as close to 50 percent, but now, as the technicians involved with IVF are becoming more skilled, the figure is much lower.

IVF pregnancies are usually supported in the early months with progesterone suppositories, and you would be monitored carefully by your doctor.

IVF research is leading to new exciting departures in reproductive medicine, and it is possible, in the future, that doctors will be able to evaluate the quality of the sperm and the ovum prior to conception. In itself, this would limit the number of miscarriages due to abnormal chromosomes from either the father or mother.

Artificial Insemination

Artificial insemination by donor (AID) does carry an increased miscarriage rate, and it makes no difference if the insemination is made with fresh or frozen sperm. Interestingly enough, sperm from your partner can cause an even higher rate of miscarriage than sperm from a donor.

Surgical Treatment of Infertility

If your fallopian tubes are damaged and you have surgery to repair them, and then conceive, there is an increased chance of miscarriage. The reasons again are unclear. But it may be that a shortened or altered tube slows down or speeds up the progress of the egg before fertilization, which may promote a less than perfect start for the conception.

Endometrial Biopsy

I described in chapter 3 (page 69) the use of an endometrial biopsy to assess whether a luteal phase defect (LPD) might be the cause of your miscarriages. The procedure is performed in the second half of your menstrual cycle, when you could unknowingly already be pregnant.

If conception has taken place and the blastocyst is already implanted in the uterus, as you might imagine, it could be scooped out by the biopsy instrument, which is inserted directly into the uterus. In fact, such a dramatic ending to a pregnancy is fortunately very rare. However, to avoid that situation it is advisable to have a pregnancy test prior to the biopsy, because the sophisticated new tests can be carried out eight days after ovulation, or on day 22 of your cycle. The endometrial biopsy would usually be performed between days 22 and 25 of the cycle. This is one case where technology has finally caught up with our needs!

Environmental Factors

The various disorders, diseases, and afflictions that might affect a mother and her fetus are sometimes visible, sometimes unseen and unexpected. But the next category includes the least definable and the most politically sensitive causes of miscarriage, which, unfortunately, are also the ones we often can do the least about. However, if your doctor can detect no other reasonable cause for your recurring miscarriages, then environmental factors may have to be taken into account.

Pollution

Very often, after contemplating becoming pregnant or undergoing the stress of conceiving and then losing a baby, we can be overcome not only by grief but also by despair at the world we live in, by the pollution and chemicals with their insidious roles in our lives, by the very water we drink and air we breathe.

Pregnancy is usually a time of great optimism, buoyed by a renewed confidence in life and humanity, by our faith in the future as we attempt to bring another person into this world. Natural fears about wars, chemical clouds hovering over us, and violence perpetrated on man and woman, by man and woman, all tend to be dissipated by the sheer magic and joy of the reproductive process.

The shadow of pollution that hangs over our environment may only begin to appear ominous if, after one or more miscarriages, you begin talking to women in your neighborhood or in the same workplace and learn that they, too, have experienced unaccountable miscarriages. Or, maybe there is a higher than usual incidence of birth defects or premature labor in those places.

What can you do? What, indeed? It is not surprising that such issues can lead even the most optimistic of us to a sense of despair. But, as usual, the energy for change tends to come from the women who have found themselves caught by life's unfairness.

If nothing else, when you do notice clusters of miscarriages, or similar birth problems, then at least you have the choice: Either you change where you work or where you live, or you get out there to lobby for change by the polluters.

Just look at some of the notable hazards of our times and the effect they have had on world opinion.

The terrible accident at the Union Carbide plant at Bhopal, India, led to the release of a cloud of methyl isocyanate gas and possibly cyanide. More than two thousand people were killed. But also miscarriages and stillbirths were reported as spin-off effects of the tragedy.

The Love Canal disaster, in New York State, was exposed when children became mysteriously ill, and when miscarriages, stillbirths, and birth defects seemed unusually high in the community. The local school, it was discovered, was built on top of a chemical dump. Metal drums containing the chemical waste had rusted, and their chemicals had been seeping into the water and soil.

When women in Oregon noticed that there was a particularly high miscarriage rate in the spring of each year, a study found that the spraying of whole areas with a herbicide containing dioxin, one of the most poisonous chemicals, was the cause. Dioxin was the ingredient in Agent Orange, used to defoliate Vietnam, which became associated with high rates of miscarriage, stillbirth, birth defects, and cancer in the returning soldiers and their families.

People in Silicon Valley, in California, recently noticed that their miscarriage rate was two or three times as high as the national average. They discovered that water had been contaminated by underground storage tanks from one silicon chip manufacturer. Sixty thousand gallons of toxic chemicals had leaked into the water table.

Research into the effects of these *reported* disasters is slow and of course underfunded. Vested interests are battling much more strongly to avoid detection of chemical dumping or exposure of workers. In terms of miscarriages, unfortunately, the fairly high spontaneous rate—recently reported as 30 percent and over in first pregnancies—tends to work against activists who try to link pollution and pregnancy loss. Who is to say it's not just chance, that the rate is higher in Arcadia Row than on the other side of town?

Yet it is obviously very important that we continue to monitor the dangers of the various chemicals and levels of radiation that have now become part of everyday life. Just recently, for example, the chlorine used to bleach the fibers in disposable diapers has been banned in Sweden, and its use is under discussion elsewhere in Britain and Europe, because the large quantities of chlorine required for their manufacture are washed into rivers and oceans. Disposable diapers? How could something so innocent pose a threat? we might ask.

Known Pollutants that Are Harmful in Pregnancy

One of the best-known hazards in pregnancy, *cigarette smoking,* affects the whole reproductive process: It tends to decrease the sperm count in men, leads to abnormal sperm, and can promote infertility as well as increase the risk of spontaneous miscarriage. The effect of smoking quite obviously restricts the blood supply to the ovaries and to the uterus. Fortunately smoking can be eliminated at least in our homes, and hopefully we can control our exposure to others' smoking at work. Maybe it's time for yellow signs, like those in the back windows of so many cars, that read Please Don't Smoke, Baby on Board!

Alcohol is associated with an increased miscarriage rate, but it is not a known *cause.* Drinking should be limited to no more than an occasional, relaxing glass of wine or beer during pregnancy—certainly not more than once a week.

Workplace Pollutants

Some sixty thousand chemicals are used commercially, of which only a handful have ever been tested for their effects on pregnancy. Most researchers, however, don't test their effect on miscarriage, but their ability to cause birth defects. Other studies involve chemicals and the associated incidence of cancer in young children. Miscarriage is a much more hidden kind of disaster.

Some chemicals such as DDT and metals such as lead, copper, and zinc interfere with the implantation of the fetus. Mercury can affect a developing embryo because it can lead to a failure to implant in the uterine lining after fertilization. Some anesthetic gases increase the rate of miscarriage in nurses working in operating rooms. Certain drugs used to fight cancer have also been linked to a high incidence of miscarriages among nurses handling the drugs. However, all such reports are from isolated studies and do not constitute proof.

With the growing number of women now in the workforce, it is time that our attitude to such hazards changes, too. The effect of various chemicals and agents is very difficult to assess during pregnancy, because of the altered physiology of the pregnant woman. For example, the amount of air breathed in pregnancy changes, and the circulatory volume is increased, which makes the assessment of those chemicals even more complex.

Women can also be affected indirectly by their partner's exposure to chemicals. He might be bringing lead dust home on his clothes, or traces of chemicals might be detected in his seminal fluid. These chemicals can be absorbed through the vaginal skin. So any man whose partner has undergone more than one miscarriage should also inquire at work about the possible reproductive risks to which he is exposed. If these risks are not initially known, then attempts should be made to obtain all the relevant information.

If you are in early pregnancy, or are planning to become pregnant, and you are worried or uncertain about the hazards at your workplace, you should discuss this with your doctor, midwife, or an occupational health physician. You might also inquire from the relevant government agencies or your employers as to the levels of risk. You might want to know if you could be removed from that working area during pregnancy, or whether you should wear protective clothing.

Here is a list of addresses and phone numbers that might help you in your investigations (from "Reproductive Hazards in the Workplace: What the Practitioner Needs to Know about Chemical Exposures," by Paul and Himmelstein, *Obstetrics and Gynecology* 71, no. 6 (1988):928).

Hot Lines

Pregnancy/Environmental Hot Line National Birth Defects Center, Kennedy Memorial Hospital, Boston: Massachusetts. Will *accept calls from practitioners nationally:* 800-322-5014; (Massachusetts only) 617-787-4957.

Pregnancy Exposure Information Service, University of Connecticut Health Center, Farmington: Connecticut only: 800-325-5391.

Washington State Poison Control Network, University of
Washington, Seattle: 800-732-6985; (Washington only)
206-526-2121.

Women working on farms and in gardens, in hospital labo-
ratories and operating rooms; women working as anesthesiolo-
gists, dentists, and dental assistants—all seem to have an
increased rate of miscarriage. Also, women working in chemical industries where rayon, glue, or plastics are made and those
who work with radiation or microchips are even more at risk
for miscarrying. Women working in the environments mentioned above should be encouraged where feasible to limit
their exposure to the offending chemicals without affecting
their position at work. If you are working among such known
hazards and cannot be moved to a safer position, you might
consider taking a temporary job away from that workplace at
least during the first four months of pregnancy, if you can
possibly arrange or afford such a break.

Changes are being instigated. For example the air in hospital operating rooms is now filtered to keep the level of anesthetic gases low. But much more attention should be paid to
this area of noxious agents or chemicals in the workplace.
Physicians must be more aware that there should be greater
enforcement of laws, such as the Occupational Safety and
Health Act, which mandates workplace safety and health for all
employees.

The most obvious, simple, and apparently innocent form
of work for women has always been office work. But now with
widespread use of video display terminals (VDTs) and photocopying machines, even this area is turning into something of
a reproductive minefield.

The VDT has become like the television, an indispensable
addition to our lives that we find hard to see as a culprit. During
the last ten years, most young adults have probably learned to
use both at work or at home. So what is the problem? Here are

some useful facts about the potential hazards of VDTs, plus some recent reports in the press about women's own perceptions and concerns.

VDTs, Radiation, and Pregnancy

It is unlikely that the fetus will come to harm from any industrial source of radiation, because levels of radiation are checked and double-checked regularly. Any person who works with lasers or with ultraviolet, infrared, or microwave radiation is monitored most closely. Harm can come to your baby only if you were to receive a severe radiation *burn.* If you work with photocopying machines, no harm will result as long as you keep the top closed when the machine is copying and do not expose yourself to the green light. (It is alarming, though, to see how lazy we have all become, not only leaving the top open, but exposing our eyes regularly to that light.)

If you work with ionizing radiation (namely X rays), you must wear a film badge to monitor the dose. These badges are usually read quarterly, and you may have access to the records. If you are planning to become pregnant, the best advice would be to request a badge reading every month to be sure the radiation dose remains safe in the period *before* conception.

The recommended, acceptable level for the embryo or fetus is 0.5 rem, or rad, which is equivalent to 1.5 rems for a pregnant woman, because of absorption of radiation by the abdominal wall, which usually reduces the fetal dose to the safe level. However, remember to add to this amount the radiation from diagnostic X rays so that the total does not exceed the safe level. Moving to a more innocuous department during your pregnancy would likely be viewed sympathetically by your boss or supervisor.

A New Study on VDTs and Pregnancy   As for VDTs, the general conclusion is that they do not emit radiation at levels that would cause a problem. However, in a recent study, researchers at the Kaiser-Permanente Medical Care Program in Oakland, California, found that women who use video display terminals for *more than twenty hours a week* in the first three months of pregnancy suffer almost twice as many miscarriages as women doing other types of office work.

The authors of the study, which was published in the June 1988 issue of the *American Journal of Industrial Medicine* and was reported in the *New York Times* on June 5, 1988, felt that their findings did not mean that the terminals *themselves* had necessarily caused the miscarriages, but that unmeasured factors such as job-related stress and poor working conditions could also have been responsible.

The study, which seemed to show more a statistical than a causal correlation, was carried out on sixteen hundred pregnant women. The researchers noted that heavy users of VDTs were also more likely to have children with birth defects, but that increase was not thought to be statistically significant.

Although people have long been guessing that there may be links between VDTs and miscarriages, this study provides the first epidemiological evidence, based on substantial numbers of pregnant VDT operators, to show the relation between higher miscarriage rates and women who work at VDTs for more than twenty hours a week (which is only four hours a day, in an average work week).

The VDT and Today's Working Woman   About fifteen million VDTs are in use in the United States as I write, and some three million more are added annually, according to *VDT News,* an industry newsletter. About half the estimated ten million people who use the machines regularly at work are women of childbearing age.

The study's findings grew out of research that was originally meant to determine the effects on pregnant women of pesticides that were being used to combat Mediterranean fruit flies in California, in 1981 and 1982. Fifteen-hundred and eighty-three pregnant women who attended three Kaiser-Permanente obstetric and gynecology clinics in northern California were surveyed.

The study found increased risks of miscarriage in both first and second trimesters of pregnancy for all women who worked with VDTs for more than the previously mentioned twenty hours a week, in comparison with nonworking women. They also found an increase of about 40 percent in birth defects among children of pregnant women who used VDTs more than five hours a week.

Why Do VDTs Affect the Fetus? Some experts have suggested that low-level electromagnetic radiation from VDTs may be able to alter or disrupt cellular development. According to *VDT News,* experiments with mice and chicks have shown such effects.

The National Institute of Occupational Safety and Health (NIOSH) has said that VDTs do not emit unsafe levels of electromagnetic radiation. But critics counter that any additional radiation either at work or at home (from smoke detectors, for example) imposes additional risks. NIOSH has identified clusters of miscarriages and other complications of pregnancy among VDT users, but no cause and effect relationship has yet been established.

There is very little published in medical journals, and no further organized epidemiological research is underway on VDTs and pregnancy. However, current research is underway at the Mount Sinai School of Medicine, in New York City, with the support of the March of Dimes, which is now taking very seriously the assumed link between VDT use and miscarriage rates. They plan to measure emissions of ionizing and electromagnetic radiation from the machines the women use and to study the configuration of their desks, chairs, and VDTs; their usage of the VDTs; and other factors such as smoking and drinking. They also plan to use questionnaires to assess individual stress levels.

The researchers at Mount Sinai will make use of very early pregnancy tests to determine the exact beginning of a pregnancy and will thus record *all* miscarriages, even those that might otherwise have gone unrecorded. As I mentioned earlier, these accurate and very early pregnancy tests will be one way for researchers to bring more exact figures to our statistical knowledge of miscarriage rates.

The effects of clusters of miscarriages in certain workplaces can lead to a sense of panic among some women. One recently reported case received some national attention, though the women involved seemed to be rational about the situation.

One story was reported in the *New York Times* by Tamar Lewin in December 1988, just six months after the report on the research into VDTs and miscarriage clusters and the effect of VDTs on birth defects, stillbirths, and premature labor. The story was about women at a major national newspaper, *USA Today.*

There had been a rash of miscarriages among women working in the newsrooms at *USA Today* headquarters in Arlington, Virginia, and while no one appeared to have any real evidence about what might be causing the miscarriages, some of the women interviewed at the paper speculated that the problem might be related to construction work in the building or to the video display terminals (VDTs) that reporters and editors use.

In the last few years, epidemiologists have investigated a dozen clusters of miscarriages among VDT users, but found no scientific evidence that the VDT, itself, caused the problems.

Allen Wilcox, epidemiologist at the National Institute of Environmental Health Sciences, North Carolina, explained in this same report, "Where there have been clusters of rare tumors in the past, it has sometimes pointed us to the discovery of the cause. But, although epidemiologists have made basic efforts to examine miscarriage clusters, miscarriage itself is so common that no one has ever determined whether any specific cluster was anything more than a statistical oddity." Dr. Wilcox was referring to the *New England Journal of Medicine* report, in the summer of 1988, that 31 percent of all conceptions are likely to end in miscarriage.

In a nutshell, this story based on women's own feelings at one specific workplace sums up the dilemma. Can we locate a genuine link between VDT users and miscarriage? Do the statistics for general miscarriage rates rule out the likelihood of such specific causes? With a 30 plus percent chance of miscarrying, anyway, women in such lines of work might be more prone to other factors such as high stress levels, advanced maternal age, or the other known causes of miscarriage. Obviously much more research needs to be performed in this area.

What Other Hazards Should You Avoid During Pregnancy?

The use of aerosol sprays should be avoided before conception and during pregnancy. Much more is now known about the effects of aerosols on the outer atmosphere, and, since alternatives to most aerosol sprays—whether deodorants, hair sprays, room deodorizers, spray polishes, or oven cleaners—are now available, it would be advisable to avoid any potential hazard.

Even though the halogenated hydrocarbons currently in use to create the propellant have *not* been implicated in causing any problem to the fetus or mother, it is always best to err on the side of caution. It is better to use the sprays containing carbon dioxide as the propellant. During pregnancy, you have an increased blood supply, which means you take in more oxygen and similarly will absorb more foreign particles from the air you breathe.

Should you need to use pesticides, for example, you would be advised to ask your husband or a friend to do the spraying, and make sure you are not in the vicinity when the spraying is taking place. Similarly, if you are painting the baby's room or redecorating your house, be careful when stripping off any old paint that might contain lead. Leave that task to others. Make sure the room is well ventilated.

Illicit Drugs

Recreational drugs should *never* be used during pregnancy. They are never pure and may have all manner of harmful effects on the baby (and mother), even leading to the baby being born an addict, for example, following heroin use. Cocaine has recently been shown to be a cause of miscarriages and to cause permanent brain damage in the baby. Amphetamines may cause major problems during pregnancy.

Can You Move to a New House?

The stress and labor of moving to a new house or apartment are often linked with miscarriages and premature labor. As I have pointed out previously, neither the psychological or emotional demands of such a move, nor the physical stress of lifting and carrying will, by themselves, trigger a miscarriage. However, it is obviously advisable, particularly if you have miscarried before, to avoid any heavy lifting or unnecessary stress. This is not one of those times to prove you are equal to men, or other women for that matter. Sit back and organize the activity from the sidelines.

Is It Safe to Use the Microwave Oven During Pregnancy?

Microwave ovens are a source of radiation, and the Food and Drug Administration (FDA) has established emission standards for any microwave appliance on the domestic market. The permissible limits are 5 milliwatts of radiation per square centimeter, measured at two inches from the oven surface. The manufacturers believe these ovens are perfectly safe for home use, whether the user is pregnant or not. And, of course, like VDTs, microwaves have become very much established as part of a modern lifestyle.

The only potential hazard lies in increasing these small levels of radiation, which should be added to the emission from a smoke detector in your house or apartment. If you use the microwave daily, be cautious; make sure you don't stay around the oven when it is in use. And certainly don't lean against it while chatting on the kitchen phone, for example. If in doubt, get someone else to do the cooking.

Should You Move Your Household Pets Out for the Pregnancy?

As I have discussed previously in the section on infections (chapter 6, page 149), toxoplasmosis can be transmitted by cats that are kept as much-loved pets. The parasitic infection is known to lead to miscarriage, premature labor, stillbirth, or birth defects. However, its incidence is very rare—about 1 in 8,000 in America today—and is a far less serious threat than is commonly thought. Most people have already picked up immunity to toxoplasmosis from living with household pets prior to their pregnancy.

It can only be transmitted if you handle the litter tray and come into direct contact with a cat's feces. So, if you still have to empty the litter tray, wear rubber gloves. And, if at all possible have someone else do the chore. Other household pets such as dogs, goldfish, birds, or even snakes do not transmit the infection. But it can be contracted from eating raw fish or meat.

You should be screened for previous exposure, to see if you have the antibodies, either before conception or when you receive a positive pregnancy test. If already pregnant and you are found to have the antibodies, then your pregnancy will be monitored very carefully. If the level of antibodies is very high, you will need to discuss with your doctor and your husband whether to continue with this pregnancy or to terminate it and treat the condition first.

Are Saunas, Hot Tubs, and Sunlamps Safe?

When your body is subjected to extreme heat over a lengthy period, you may become overheated (hyperthermic), which could adversely affect the fetus. There is no direct link between such usage and miscarriage, but if you are at all concerned, you would be advised against using saunas, steam rooms, or hot tubs while pregnant, or you may be advised to restrict their use to very short periods.

Sunlamps have a strong association with an increase in skin cancer, for they expose the body to unusually high levels of ultraviolet radiation. They have not been specifically linked with miscarriage or birth defects. However, as there are still the dangers of overheating your body, and no one has any information of possible long-term effects on the fetus or the pregnancy, my advice would be to discontinue their use in pregnancy.

Can Watching TV Be Hazardous to a Pregnancy?

Television rays, even from color televisions, have *not* been shown to be a form of ionizing radiation, so television watching should not be harmful, not even sitting close to a television set for long periods. The only danger would be to your back if you tend to sit slumped for hours on a sofa in front of the set. You would be best advised to sit on a firm chair, so your back is supported, with your feet up on a low stool, to maximize circulation and ease potential lower back problems.

PART THREE

Are You Ready to Try Again?

8

Why Is Healthy Grieving So Important?

WHATEVER anyone else says or how they respond to you, the first thing to bear in mind is that the death of your baby is a profound tragedy. Whether you lose a baby before or shortly after birth, you will be going through an emotionally devastating time. If you miscarried a baby in the very early weeks, your grief may be compounded by the fact that no one else knew you were pregnant, other than your husband and maybe your doctor. And because there were no visible signs, your sadness may be seen as inappropriate. "Have another baby quickly" will be their best advice. "Cheer up, you can get pregnant again."

Indeed, until recently, miscarriage was treated as an isolated medical condition or "mistake." The fetus would be hurriedly taken away, without a chance for you to hold, touch, or maybe even know its sex. You would be put back on the gynecological ward, out of sight and hearing of other babies crying or of mothers holding their new infants. You would be discharged from the hospital and told to see your doctor when next you became pregnant.

Only now have doctors, and allied medical professionals, come to appreciate the tremendous emotional impact of a miscarriage; its impact on you as a couple, and its impact on family, friends, and other children at home. This form of treatment of women who had suffered a loss of pregnancy, or of an infant, quite often led to severe psychological reactions; as the mother became obsessed with what her body had produced, or preoccupied with her guilt and sense of betrayal by her own body.

She may well have spent months, if not years, in a morbid state of unresolved grief. As so often happens, women were left with their sadness, guilt, fear of inadequacy and failure, struggling alone with these feelings when really the situation was simply out of their own control.

Now you will find hospital staff and your own doctor genuinely upset by your loss and sensitized to your very natural and necessary grieving process.

The American College of Obstetricians and Gynecologists (ACOG) has produced a very helpful pamphlet called *After Your Baby Dies.* You should be given something of this nature, either by your doctor or the hospital social workers, to read.

At the Mount Sinai Hospital, where I work, the special perinatal social workers who care for the problems of bereaved parents give out a booklet called *Miscarriage, Stillbirth, and Infant Death: Understanding Grief and Coping with a Loss,* which was written by the coordinator of the Pregnancy Loss Peer Support Program, which is run by the New York section of the National Council of Jewish Women, and by two Mount Sinai social workers, Virginia Walther and Amy Carter.

Why Grieving Is Normal and Healthy

With the loss of a baby, you will never forget that the child was part of you, meant so much to you. Even if he or she had only been a dream in your mind, the baby had already become an important member of your family, an extension of yourselves. The scar left by the loss will never vanish, but you want to come to the point where you can remember your lost baby comfortably and realistically.

You should expect to run through a gamut of emotions: pure grief, sadness, a lot of uncontrolled crying, guilt, anger, depression, maybe fear of any ambivalence you felt toward the pregnancy; a lot of blaming yourself, your partner, or even the doctor and hospital. Also there will be a profound sense of loss that may bring out other losses in your life such as that of a recently lost parent, friend, or even your long years of experience with infertility.

Your first stage in the grieving process will likely be that of *shock and denial.* You may just feel stunned and numb, unable to believe what has happened. If it was a very early loss, the pregnancy might now seem unreal, as though you had imagined the whole condition. The emotions of shock and denial actually serve to help us through an overly stressful time, giving us time to come to terms with the reality.

As you develop more awareness and begin to accept the reality, you may begin to develop *somatic complaints* such as an emptiness in the stomach or chest, or a heaviness around the throat. Headaches, sleeping problems, loss of appetite, severe depression—these are all normal reactions. Of course, if milk comes into your breasts, you will feel a profound yearning for the baby you never got to hold or to feed. Your breasts will ache, along with your heart. If the loss occurred much later in the pregnancy, when you were already used to feeling the baby kicking, it is quite common to go on feeling that kicking, those lingering sensations. Hearing a baby's cry may bring on terrible crying spurts. Seeing other women with babies can bring out intense anger and more pain.

You may well begin to feel afraid that you're going crazy, as your mind struggles to deal with confused feelings and emotions. Somehow, you have to hang on to your sense of self, and release the anger and the pain.

If it is possible to hold a funeral or memorial service for the dead baby, this might help in bringing on a time of *restitution,* as you get to say good-bye to your lost child. It is important to use the name you were going to call the child, to talk about him or her as a real person. Friends and relatives may still find it hard to discuss your loss with you. They will be afraid of bringing back all that grief and of seeing you cry, but if you talk openly and name the baby, then it will be harder for them to ignore what has happened and to utter clichés, such as, "Don't worry, you can always have another."

You don't replace one child with another, just as you'd never replace a dead mother with a substitute. You must allow yourself to talk about the baby and open up to others.

You may find you don't want to go out of the house and that you avoid social occasions because it is just too difficult to deal with people, their questions, and their insensitivity. At home you will be battling with the void that is now in your life and the terrible awareness of the finality of the loss.

Very likely, you will want to see your doctor to hear reasons and explanations that will help you come to terms with the tragedy. You will still be feeling responsible for the loss yourself. In order to get back to normal daily life, you will need to feel you can share some of that burden in an effort to assuage the guilt.

And slowly, very slowly, you might feel you can embrace the loss and face the future again. At this stage, communication with your husband should be open and nonaccusatory, loving and giving; then maybe you will be ready to try for another baby.

But there are other issues involved, too, apart from your secret inner grieving. There are so many interconnected social consequences. Carol Goldman, one of the excellent perinatal social workers I referred to briefly at the beginning of this chapter, who works with bereaved parents at the Mount Sinai Hospital, shared with me some of the lessons she has learned from her work with newly bereaved parents.

Feelings the Mother Should Expect to Experience

Apart from those feelings connected with a pure sense of grief, there may be other more conflicting emotions that will be stewing inside you.

> *Loss of self-esteem:* How are you going to face the world now? How will you deal with your coworkers, parents, and parents-in-law who were all looking forward to this baby?
>
> *Isn't it your fault?*
>
> *Is it a sign of your inadequacy as a woman?*
>
> *Helplessness:* After all, this was out of your control. You ate well, read the right books, tried to lead a healthy good life before conception and during the pregnancy. So what went wrong?
>
> *Loss of control:* This is very hard to deal with, especially if you are used to a level of success and competency in your life and work.
>
> *Uncomfortable feelings about your body:* Is there something wrong with you? Why did your body betray you? You may feel like a stranger in your own skin, like you no longer understand how your body operates.

Special Feelings if the Miscarriage Was in the Early Weeks

This can sometimes prove to be the hardest form of loss, as you might not have even told friends and colleagues yet that you were pregnant. Now you have nothing to show for your loss. No one will be sympathetic. You may have gone through a horrific experience, with sudden blood loss and painful cramping, terrifying hours at home when your doctor said, "Just go to bed. It will probably be all right." Who will be able to share that with you?

Maybe you miscarried at home alone, on the toilet. All your dreams and hopes flushed cruelly away in a sea of blood. It is hard to banish those images from your mind.

Maybe you carried what you felt was the fetus in a little container, in your bag, on the subway, bus, or in your car, to the doctor's office. What a strange world to have entered.

Special Feelings if the Fetus Was Lost after the Twentieth Week

You may have had to experience induction of labor, only to produce a dead baby. Your doctor probably advised you to take medication to help ease the pain of the miscarriage or delivery, but you can't help feeling guilty that that was what killed your baby (even though it had *no* chance of survival on its own once born so prematurely).

Depending on the attitude of the hospital and nurses, you may have emerged not only empty armed, but seething with anger—as some of the women have already described in this book—at the way both you and the dead baby were treated.

If you had been in the hospital or at home on complete bed rest, now you wouldn't be able to escape terrible feelings of failure and frustration at being incapable of producing a child.

Lying in the hospital bed, not daring to move a fraction in case you set off the miscarriage, can be a terrifying and emotionally devastating experience that few other people will ever undergo.

Doing nothing is the best thing you can do. But how much of nothing is humanly possible?

Were You Able to See and Hold the Baby?

Often parents are afraid to see or hold their dead baby, because they imagine that the child will look dreadful; they even imagine him looking like a monster. You may find yourself saying, "I'd rather picture the baby in my mind as if she were alive." But according to Carol Goldman, it really is best if at all possible to see your baby, otherwise you might later develop distorted notions of the birth and the real nature of the child. These images can lead to worse feelings, which might crowd out the rather idealized picture you hoped to hold on to.

The fact is that, despite their fears, most mothers and fathers are relieved and pleased when they do see or hold their baby. The hospital nurses or the social worker will bring him or her to you, either dressed in clothes you provided or wrapped in a receiving blanket, maybe wearing a hat to protect the head. The baby's actual appearance, as if asleep, will be far more comforting than any fantasy you could have created.

If you are still undecided, the hospital could take a photograph of the baby. Even if you refuse to see the picture at the time, they will hold onto that photograph for several months in case you change your mind.

Do you want to hold the baby? Think it over. It can be very helpful just to feel the baby against your aching chest, to give yourself and your husband time to say those good-byes. You can let the nurse know if you want her to stay or if you'd prefer to be left alone. (See Figure 12.)

PERINATAL BEREAVEMENT REFERRAL & CHECKLIST

Mother's Name: _____   Date of Delivery: _____

Father"s Name: _____   Gestational Age: _____

Address: _____   Sex of Infant: _____ Weight: _____

_____   Previous Perinatal Loss: Yes ___ NO ___

Phone #: _____   How many _____

Relevant Medical History: _____

_____

_____

_____

	ACCEPTED	NOT ACCEPTED
1. Saw baby: Mother: Father:		
2. Touched and/or held baby Mother: Father:		
3. Parents' available support systems contacted: Relative: Friend: Clergy:		
4. Autopsy consent signed Yes: No:		
5. Bereavement Booklet given to parent(s)		
6. Polaroid Photo Taken: Yes: No:		
7. Polaroid photo given to parent(s) Yes: No:		
8. Copy of footprints given to parent(s) Yes: No:		

9. Summary of grief reaction or RN's special concerns:

Referral to Social Work Made: Yes: No: Date Referred:		
Patient was transferred to:		

_____
Primary Nurse   3/89

Figure 12.   Bereavement Referral & Checklist Form.

Another very helpful booklet, *When Hello Means Good-bye,* is produced by an Oregon-based group (you will find them listed in the Resource section, page 223) called Perinatal Loss. I would like to bring to you the firsthand account they published of a mother and father's time spent with the baby they had just lost.

Hello, Little Son,

I was so afraid to finally meet you. When you died two days ago inside of me, I was afraid you would not be someone I could recognize and know. Forgive my fears.

The first thing I notice are the birth bruises that any prematurely born infant might have. And there is so much blond hair on your little head. David put a little stocking cap on your head to hide the molding of your skull bones. I know it is a change that comes with death, but also that it's because you are small and were born before your time. Your eyes are closed and puffy. If only you would look up at me. Your mouth is open, with a crimson color to your lips. David thinks you look a lot like your brother. It takes two hands to hold your limp head and body. It is a perfect little body, warm and soft with all the right number of fingers and toes.

Your color almost looks pink and white except for the bruises and a little vernix on your face and hair. Because everything is so perfect, it is painfully difficult to understand what went wrong. Such a big boy you are—5 pounds and 8 ounces. We supposed you would only be 3 or 4 pounds, coming so soon. And the size of your hands and feet! You don't feel so little as I hold you close.

You are just the right size. There is pain and pleasure in knowing your body, the knees and feet that kicked. We can hold you once, bathe you, dress you. And then we'll say good-bye, keeping only the memory of you and some mementoes.

Your body will soon be gone, but the love goes on forever.

Have You Named the Baby?

Give your baby a name, preferably the one you had been planning for this child all along. Don't "save" that name for your next child, as it rightly belongs to this one. Names are important and will help you talk about this child to others. You will use it when you talk about this baby to your other children or to your family. Memories become firmer when you have a name and face to hold onto.

Keepsakes and Mementoes

One of the worst days of your life will be leaving the hospital
empty armed, with nothing to hold onto. If your miscarriage
was early, you will have only the sense of loss and emptiness
inside to see you through. It is hard then to talk about keeping
mementoes. But, if the baby was delivered, then you should be
able to collect some reminders to take home. Not all hospitals
will automatically think of letting you do this, so make a point
of asking. For example, you might want to keep

- a lock of hair (though not all babies will be born with
  hair)
- a set of footprints and handprints (these can be done for
  even the earliest miscarriages)
- a birth certificate, or certificate issued by the hospital
  (see Figure 13)
- a picture of your baby
- the plastic arm bracelet prepared by the hospital to identify your child

Our baby _____ was delivered at

The Mount Sinai Medical Center on _____
                                          (Date)

                                                          AM
at _____ PM

Sex _____ Weight _____

Parents:
Mother _____

Father _____

Physician _____

Attended by Clergy _____

To obtain any legal document regarding your baby, please contact the
Department of Health, 125 Worth Street, New York, New York 10013

Figure 13.   Mount Sinai Medical Center birth
certificate.

- a small scrap of paper from the fetal-monitor showing a tracing of your baby's heart rate
- a record of the weight, length, head, and chest measurements of your baby
- the receiving blanket your baby was first wrapped in
- a flower from the bouquet brought in by your partner that when dried and kept in the photograph album will have special meaning

These are only suggestions for you and your partner, at a time when it will be hard to think rationally. Yet, if you leave the hospital without making your feelings known, without collecting your mementoes, you may regret it later.

Besides, performing some of these physical and practical tasks may help satisfy a degree of that intense, and unsatisfied, need to care for your baby you may now be experiencing.

One of the cruelest ironies is that even though your baby is dead, your need to cradle, nurture, and speak lovingly toward him or her does not diminish.

Can Grieving Really Help Overcome the Pain?

Now let me turn to Philippa, whom we met briefly in the opening chapter of the book, and how the toll of five miscarriages, all those losses and deaths, swept her unwillingly through a door leading to a very different kind of world.

Normally, Philippa is a woman others might envy: tall and beautiful, with a mane of strawberry blond hair, she is married to a kind, loving man and has a bright pretty daughter of eleven. The family lives in an elegant brownstone in mid-Manhattan, and they have a country house on Long Island. Artworks adorn their walls, history books their shelves. Philippa involves herself with charity work. It's a comfortable, one would say, privileged existence, except that Philippa has a dark side to her soul. Just recently, she experienced the fifth miscarriage late in the second trimester, at around the 23rd week. Each time has been more devastating than the last. Within her story lies, firsthand, much of the material I have been discussing in this chapter. Just how can miscarriage best be handled by the hospital? Does the grieving process really work?

"We Were Able to Cry and to Hold Her."

On my second miscarriage, at 21 weeks, I asked to see the baby, because I knew it had lived for a few minutes. He was a little boy, strong and beautiful. It shocked me to see him—he was 12 inches long, like a doll, a perfectly formed miniature baby. He looked fine. In fact, I wanted to give him artificial respiration. I just knew he wanted to live. But none of the efforts made could save him. They said he was too young to keep alive. The doctors tried hard to be helpful, but they were really trying in vain.

Eventually, the baby just stopped breathing in my arms. It was a very painful experience. Neither my husband nor I really knew what to do. A nurse came back in and she put a nice blanket around him. Then she took him away; but we never knew where he was taken or buried. I do wish we'd been more prepared, or had someone there to advise us. I would have liked to bury the child, but I just wasn't emotionally ready to start asking such questions.

I miscarried another pregnancy, again at 23 weeks. Then, on my fourth attempt at pregnancy, although the membranes ruptured at the 24th week, I was given steroids to help mature the baby's lungs in case he was born alive and could be treated.

Well, he was breathing and was born weighing just under 2 pounds, and 14 inches long. He was a very strong little boy, delivered by C-section. Usually C-sections are seldom done at that stage of pregnancy but, if you're trying for viability, it is the least stressful way of delivery. I had had all the risks read out to me: that only 1 in 10 survives at 24 weeks; and I was told about the problems for babies kept in neonatal care units. But my husband and I made the decision because to us 24 weeks seemed so close to the viable age, and I just didn't want to have to go through all this again.

The staff in the neonatal unit were very excited. His brain

appeared to be in good shape, because he had not had an intracranial bleed. They fed him little bottles and I pumped my milk. He began to develop a bowel problem, which they corrected surgically. But the anesthesia was very stressful, and after that he developed breathing difficulties. One day he'd be up, the next down. It was agony, a nightmare existence. I'd stayed in the hospital myself for a week, as I was bleeding and unwell. My husband and I visited the neonatal care unit every day. During the last week we were there night and day.

Our poor daughter, who was then six years old, was very confused as to what was going on. It really has all been very hard on her. We asked her if she'd like to come and see him, but she was afraid, because she'd heard he had all those tubes wired into him.

He died in his sixth week. We christened him, and had him buried ourselves with a nice service. It had been worth the struggle, because there was no brain damage. I met many other mothers in that unit, and the pain they were going through was unbelievable. The nurses were great and the obstetrician was kind and kept calling me. The hospital offered no psychological help, no support. Once a social worker dropped by to see me and said that because she was uncomfortable with death, she'd prefer not to have to deal with me!

I really did feel the lack of someone to talk to after his death. People don't know how to respond. Not that I'd have known before either. I've had friends cross the street rather than have to face me. People preferred to pretend that the baby had never happened. I had someone say to me, "I'm sorry about your little mishap." He was a *person.* We registered his birth. At least the city helped us on that; they sent the birth certificate and at six weeks they sent a death certificate. They acknowledged he was a person. And the insurance company certainly knew it. He came to $40,000 worth of bills! The "little mishap" had quite a dossier.

His death took me a year to get over; not that you're ever really over it. He was my child. I never knew how to explain to people what had happened. You can have very strange reactions that you would not have been able to predict. At home I could not do anything, and certainly could not concentrate. Whatever energy was left, had to go to my daughter. We both worked at giving her as much love and understanding as we could. I talked to her and drew pictures of it all, because I was imagining her thoughts must be quite frightening. I also didn't want her to feel that it was her fault. But she seemed mostly concerned about me. Would I ever be normal again? She wanted me back to being the fun-loving mother.

After the baby's death, I just didn't want to become pregnant again. I have a great husband and a lovely daughter. We have a nice life together. So why was I putting myself through all this misery? I was thirty-six and I'd begun to feel old. Then, I suddenly became pregnant from one night's carelessness, because I hadn't used the diaphragm. I wanted to think it had some meaning, that this was meant to be. I had heard of another team of doctors, so I thought I would give them a try. We felt most encouraged because their attitude was different and they really seemed willing to go that extra mile.

At 7 weeks of this pregnancy, the new doctor put in a suture. I was also put on progesterone and on bed rest. So I took it very easy, though I did have an amniocentesis just in case there were problems. We found out then it was a girl, and we began to feel excited. My daughter named the little girl.

But, at 20 weeks, the membranes were beginning to push through again. I was kept in the hospital and lay there flat on my back, not daring to move or hardly to breathe for three weeks. But the cervix pulled back away from the suture. The membranes burst, and once again I was in labor. It was all over at the end of the 23rd week. I think she died at the time of the birth.

It was so very painful for both of us. I suppose we were prepared to lose her, but we had deluded ourselves as well. They wrapped the baby up for us. She was so pretty and it was nice to be able to see her. You do want to know this is not some "monster" of a child. She had a very tranquil look on her face. We were able to cry and to hold her. Eventually, after we'd been with her for an hour, they took her gently away.

You need that initial time of privacy. Then the social worker at this hospital came by and really talked with us. Also, the doctor did not distance himself. You could see he felt deeply. There was a very real human quality to him that I found helpful. We felt much more supported. We made arrangements to bury her and gave her a little graveside ceremony. She's buried next to her brother.

We'll probably continue trying for a healthy pregnancy. With our new doctor, and the support of the hospital team, I do feel there is yet hope. But we'll never forget our babies that were part of our lives for such a short time.

Philippa's story brings up other points about the unfortunate experience of multiple miscarriages:

Can the baby be buried, and how do you go about that?

What can the husband or father do to help?

How do you cope with the feelings of other siblings?

How will your body react to the miscarriage?

One of the cruelest aspects of the postmiscarriage experience is that your body exhibits the same kinds of physical changes as those you would have had after the birth of a live full-term baby. Let me give you the hard facts of what you can expect. At least if you are mentally prepared, the pain may be alleviated.

Your Body Does Not Know the Baby Did Not Survive

If your miscarriage occurred late, it is likely that milk will come into your breasts. This can be painful, as you might become engorged. Your doctor might prescribe estrogen or bromo-criptine to take away the milk supply; though using cold compresses and wearing tight bras may be all that is necessary.

You will also bleed vaginally. This discharge of blood is called the *lochia* that follows delivery for up to six weeks. If it becomes very heavy, with clots, or painful or goes on beyond three or four weeks, then do let your doctor know. Any fever should also be reported to your doctor.

Postmiscarriage Depression

Even mothers who give birth to term, live-born babies are susceptible to postpartum depression. And you will be no different except that in your case, the depression is likely to be worse, as you have suffered real loss, thwarted hopes and desires. The cause of the depression is not known, but major hormonal changes are occurring within the body.

The effects of postpartum depression can be quite dramatic for some women, and you should not underestimate your own reaction. When the hormone levels drop in that rapid way, they may also affect your brain hormone levels, which control mood and basic personality. So, if you find yourself with wildly fluctuating mood changes, uncontrolled crying, anxiety attacks, strange crazy feelings, this might all be part of a typical postpartum response. Or, if your mood slumps into one of despair, because of your loss, if your self-esteem is at rock-bottom and basically you are afraid of your own condition, then do seek help from your doctor or professional counselor.

What Can You Expect Your Partner to Be Feeling?

Without being too general, or unfair on men, fathers who have just experienced miscarriage tend to be more reluctant to openly express their grief. It is common for the man involved to feel he has to keep control of himself, to be the strong one, so he can support and help his partner through her grief.

Unfortunately, for the couple, this type of attitude can be interpreted by the mother as being cold and unfeeling. You might think he didn't really care about the baby. Maybe, you wonder, he didn't really want a baby. Many men say, "I've got to be strong for her." When, of course, what they really mean is they don't want to give way to their own emotions or be seen as weak.

Some men will upset their partner even more by making comments such as, "This wasn't really a baby; it's not a great loss. We'll have another one." By talking in this way, they are reinforcing what others may also be saying. The gap between the couple's attitudes can widen, developing perhaps into serious marital problems, especially if there are other domestic pressures.

Even physical violence can emerge, because the man is trying hard to grapple with his own feelings of inadequacy and failure, while deep-down he feels unexpressed guilt. He may feel it is his fault, particularly if his wife has had a child by a previous partner. Unable to come to terms with what this means to his masculinity, he might resort to scenes of rage or violence. And, of course, for any couple involved with miscarriage, there are the joint dashed hopes of the "perfect" family, the dreamed-of happy threesome or foursome. The shared dreams of walks in the park, trips to the baseball game, birthdays, Christmases and Thanksgivings, all as a real "family."

Fathers also tend to be left to deal with the practical issues and decisions. If there is to be a burial, the planning may fall on his shoulders. If there are younger siblings at home, he will be forced into a caring and sympathetic role to support them through the crisis, while running the household and even arranging visits to the hospital. At the same time he will have his own grief to deal with.

One of the most painful ironies a father may have to confront will be receiving the hospital bills for this birth that has not brought them the much-wanted baby.

Helping Your Other Children Cope with the Loss

You should consult your pediatrician on how best to deal with siblings. You might instinctively feel you want to protect your other children from the sadness of this lost pregnancy or from the death of an infant. But, remember that avoiding discussion may make your child at home feel more, not less, upset. He or she will be sensitive to your moods anyway and will wonder why he or she has been left out. A simple honest explanation that reassures them of their own safety is the most helpful.

Younger children can feel guilt, as Philippa described. For example, the child might have been secretly wishing the new baby wouldn't take up so much of Mommy's time, then the sudden death will make her feel she has brought this about.

The way children talk about or express their feelings depends on their age and stage of development. For example, a five year old was told Mommy was pregnant, that a little sister or brother was growing in her tummy. When he heard that the baby was gone, he asked his mother *where* the baby had gone. The mother replied that the hospital would be looking after the baby. A year later, when they were driving by the hospital, the little boy suddenly said, "Can we go and see the baby now?"

Many parents find it easier to wait for the child to bring up the subject, worrying about his or her response to the idea of death. Certainly you don't have to go into detail about death, but it is best to approach the subject yourself, and then not to use explanations like, "We lost the baby." To a three year old, that might mean it will soon be found. Similarly, don't say, "The baby was sick and died," or "The baby is sleeping." Such words could play into the imagination of a young child who will then fear going to sleep or getting sick. You will have to reassure your young child that *nothing* he did or thought made the baby die.

With a child older than four years, you should encourage looking at a photograph of the baby. And if the child is about eight years old and you are going to have a funeral, you might want to let the child come along.

Remember, as Philippa mentioned, elder children living through the experiences of multiple miscarriages may fear losing *you,* that something will happen to you.

Watching you rush to the emergency room several times,

witnessing the tears, your sadness and depression, will be hard on them. So do try to be as positive in your discussion of birth and death as possible.

How Family and Friends Can Help

Family and friends should be encouraged to take an active, helpful role. Both you and your husband will be going through emotional turmoil, during which time it is hard to make decisions. You need one friend, or family member, to take over the burden of making phone calls or sending out cards to those who need to know the news. If you try to do this, you will only become upset each time you begin a new phone conversation. So if someone offers to help, ask them to take over that role for you.

From your point of view, explain to your friends that you are going to miss this baby very badly, and that you do not wish to think right now of getting pregnant again. First, you want time to mourn the child you have lost. You might even suggest they read some helpful literature!

Old friends who have not experienced this particular pain may not be very helpful at this time. Once you are back home, you might feel the need to seek out a support group made up of parents who have gone through the same tragedy as you have, who can provide real support, understanding, compassion, and respect for your feelings. The names and addresses of such groups are listed in the Resource section, page 223.

Professional counseling can also help to relieve your pain, guilt, and depression, to help you understand and accept what has happened. You may wish to seek counseling just for yourself, for both you and your partner, or, if another child is seriously disturbed, for the whole family. Think about counseling if you find, for example that (1) you are *stuck* in one phase of the grief process, so that you are having trouble working through certain problems alone or with your partner; or (2) severe physical or emotional problems are preventing you from functioning, such as being able to return to work, to care about your health and appearance, from sleeping, or getting out of bed in the morning.

Arranging a Funeral or Memorial Service

Following a miscarriage, parents are usually still in shock from their unexpected loss. But, if the baby was lost around the 15th week or later, they may have to decide whether they want a funeral or another type of ceremony. Your doctor, nurse, or social worker will speak with you about these matters. You may choose to talk with your family clergyman or with the hospital chaplain of your faith about the loss and about burial practices and rituals, as they vary among the different denominations.

If your baby was miscarried in the early weeks, so there can be no burial, you may wish to create a ritual or a memorial service to say good-bye to the child. For some parents, it can be a great comfort to have family and friends acknowledge the life and death of their baby, and to express their sorrow at a special service.

You may wish to contact a funeral home for burial or cremation. This is a distressing responsibility that a friend or family member can take on for you. A simple ceremony, with a little casket, can be comforting for you. It will mean that in the future, you have a gravesite to visit. Some towns now have a shared gravesite for miscarried babies.

The hospital should provide you with the basic information. If you do not make your own private arrangements, and if the baby was born fully formed from about the 15th week, they will arrange for its cremation and city burial (usually without charge) in an individual coffin, but it will be in a city burial plot. You will not be notified of the burial site or the day of burial.

As Your Feelings Gradually Return to Normal

There will be days when you'll wonder if your mood and sense of optimism will ever return. For most of us it does. And then you will slowly begin to feel ready to start again, with a new pregnancy. The following passage, which is also from the booklet *When Hello Means Good-bye,* shows how that change does slowly take place.

"Where is your baby?" Until yesterday, the joyful, expectant look that accompanied the question started me crying. It's only today, one month later, that I can reply, with peace in my heart, that our baby is gone, that he died before he was born.

Physically I am healed. My body has forgotten the pregnancy, but my mind is still letting go. The empty, sad feelings have lessened, and there are more times when it is possible to laugh or just to feel at peace. Getting to sleep at night is easier now than it was that first week. But fixing meals and eating them is still a chore. I've learned that eating sugar or consuming alcoholic beverages or skipping meals can bring my mood crashing to the floor. The anger I didn't feel so much at first now comes out suddenly in the form of irritability with David and the kids, especially when I am tired. Fortunately I have taken time off from work to just take care of myself.

Both writing down how I feel in my journal and exercising regularly help me to get through the day without being overwhelmed by my feelings of depression and anger. I talk for hours with friends, totally unaware of the time passing. Right now there is only one reality, loss and grief. The greeting card companies and people in general expect that each day will get a little easier and a little brighter for people in my situation. But that's not exactly how grief works. For me the days are unpredictable. Some days it seems like every woman I see is pregnant or carrying a newborn baby. *It's just so unfair.* On other days I remember vividly what Tony looked like, and I feel again the love and peace we shared at his birth.

Loving Tony has brought David and me closer. I am so grateful we can share this burden. I am told that time will heal the grief, but now I know that it is taking the time to grieve that heals.

Are You Ready to Try for Another Pregnancy?

As I mentioned in chapter 1 (page 11), the only medical factor to consider is the presence of pregnancy hormones (human chorionic gonadotropin), which, until about the third week after a miscarriage, could produce a positive pregnancy test. It is advisable, therefore, to wait until you have had your next period, sometime in the following four to six weeks, after which all the hormones will have disappeared. Then if you feel ready, you can try to conceive.

As for the psychological factors I have been discussing, only you as a couple can evaluate them. Some researchers point out that, if you conceive very quickly, you may find yourself still going through intense grieving for the lost baby—for example, around the time of its expected due date—at a time when you should be making a healthy relationship with the next baby.

You could ask yourselves questions, like those that follow, to see whether you are in fact ready.

How do you feel about holding or seeing other people's babies?

What do you feel when you see other pregnant women?

What will it be like for you to return to the same hospital?

What do you feel like walking through the baby departments?

Can you sense a difference between how you were feeling a month after your miscarriage and how you are feeling now?

Do you have more control over the unexpected weepiness?

Have you sought support or really been able to talk over your feelings with someone who understands?

That's not to say you have to be completely free of pain, anger, or resentment before planning another pregnancy. But it is advisable to keep the level of anxiety and obsessional thinking down to a reasonable level.

Coping with the Next Pregnancy

The next pregnancy will be a time of very high anxiety, especially in getting past that particular *week* (or those different weeks) when you suffered your loss or losses. You will regularly go into states of panic. There will be agonizing moments in the bathroom when you check yourself for signs of staining, or worry that gas pains are cramping.

I would like to offer the following advice to ease you through as painlessly as possible:

1. Talk to your doctor. Make sure he is prepared to listen to your fears, and to talk to you honestly about the problems, and hope, involved.
2. Request ultrasound scans to reassure yourself at regular intervals that the baby is all right, even if the scans are not required for medical reasons.

You may want to talk about a future pregnancy with a social worker or psychotherapist, so you can come to some compromise with yourself about what is reasonable in terms of *anxiety levels.* You do not want to face nine months of constant worrying. Some doctors advise setting aside a certain hour each day for worry. Then try and put the panic to one side for the rest of the day. Be prepared to rest more, even to start complete bed rest if it is felt advisable.

Think as positively as possible. Concentrate on doing everything possible to produce a healthy baby. Your doctor is aware of all the latest information, and you can rely on his medical skill. Many, many women—as you have read in this book—do come out of the long dark tunnel, even after several miscarriages, with a beautiful, healthy, full-term baby.

I wish you luck. I know that you, too, can achieve a successful pregnancy and will one day be holding your baby in your loving and welcoming arms.

Resources

A WIDE VARIETY of groups nationwide offer self-help parent support and sometimes publish their own newsletter or relevant literature; information relating to specific problems with reproduction and childbirth; or counseling services for bereavement or miscarriage. This list in no way pretends to be comprehensive. But, if you can find no outlet in your area, this list should at least give you leads for making local contacts.

Parent Support Groups

National Self-Help Clearinghouse
CUNY Graduate Center, 1206A
33 West 42nd Street
New York, NY 10036
(212) 840-1259

223

Provides the best means of finding national self-help, mutual-aid groups.

SHARE, c/o Sister Jane Marie Lamb
Saint John's Hospital
800 East Carpenter Street
Springfield, IL 62769
(217) 544-6464, ext. 5275

Provides a list of national groups for parents who have experienced miscarriage, stillbirth, or newborn loss.

The Compassionate Friends, Inc.
P.O. Box 3696
Oak Brook, IL 60522-3696
(313) 323-5010

Provides a list of self-help groups for bereaved parents who can help each other, following infant loss or the loss of an older child.

Pregnancy-Loss Peer-Support Program
National Council of Jewish Women (New York Section)
9 East 69th Street
New York, NY 10021
(212) 535-5900, ext. 16

A nonsectarian support service for parents who have suffered pregnancy loss or stillbirth. Parent support groups meet weekly for six weeks and are facilitated by trained volunteers who have also experienced pregnancy loss. Telephone counseling is also available.

Bereavement Clinic
c/o Sharon Pentel
Downstate Medical Center
450 Clarkson Avenue
Brooklyn, NY 11203
(718) 270-1189

Offers monthly support groups, led by a professional, for parents who have suffered stillbirth or infant death.

Pastoral Care
c/o Sister Mary Alice
Mercy Hospital
North Village Avenue
Rockville Center, NY 11570
(516) 255-2241

A bereavement group that meets twice monthly, for eight to ten weeks, for parents who have suffered miscarriage or stillbirth.

Pregnancy and Infant Loss Center
1415 East Wayzata Blvd, # 22
Wayzata, MN 55391
(612) 473-9372/ 24-hour helpline (612) 292-1184

A nonprofit organization offering support, resources, and education on miscarriage, stillbirth, and infant death; publishes a newsletter, "Loving Arms."

Reach Out to Parents of an Unknown Child
c/o Health House
555 North Country Road
Saint James, NY 11780
(516) 862-6743

Offers voluntary support groups of parents who have experienced unexpected loss through miscarriage, stillbirth, or infant death. Groups also available for a subsequent pregnancy. Telephone contacts available.

RESOLVE, Inc.
5 Water Street
Arlington, MA 02174
(617) 643-2424

A nonprofit organization offering counseling, referral, and support groups to people with problems of infertility and miscarriage. Telephone counseling available. Based in Boston, RESOLVE has forty-six affiliated chapters nationwide.

COPING
Santa Barbara Birth Resource Center
2255 Modoc Road
Santa Barbara, CA 93101
(805) 682-7529

Their goal is to offer comfort to people suffering intrauterine and neonatal grief; provides support for those who are experiencing a loss and for those planning or going through a subsequent pregnancy.

UNITE (Understanding Newborns in Traumatic Experiences)
Jeannes Hospital
7600 Central Avenue
Philadelphia, PA 19111
(215) 728-2082, or -3777

Offers support groups for parents who have experienced miscarriage or infant death within the area. For copies of their quarterly newsletter, send $5 to Department of Social Services, at the address above.

ICU (Intensive Caring Unlimited)
c/o Diane Sweeney
1844 Patricia Avenue
Willow Grove, PA 19090

Offers support groups for parents of children born premature or at high risk, or for those who have lost a child. They publish a newsletter and send out a packet of reprint articles for parents who have experienced miscarriage, stillbirth, and loss of a baby or child.

DAD (Depression after Delivery)
Contact: Nancy Berchtold
P.O. Box 1282
Morrisville, PA 19067
(215) 295-3994

Offers parent support groups for those experiencing postpartum depression or depression after miscarriage or infant loss. Nationwide referral service. Telephone counseling available.

Grieving Process Group
Booth Maternity Center
6051 Overbrook Avenue
Philadelphia, PA 19131
(215) 878-7800, ext. 658

Other Related Support Groups and Services

Sudden Infant Death Syndrome (SIDS)
  Regional Center
School of Social Welfare
HSC L2 Room 099
SUNY at Stony Brook
Stony Brook, NY 11794
(516) 246-2582

SIDS Counseling Program
520 First Avenue
New York, NY 10016
(212) 868-8854

National SIDS Clearinghouse
1555 Wilson Boulevard, #600
Rosslyn, VA 22209,
(703) 528-8480

Bereavement and Loss Center of New York
170 East 83d Street
New York, NY 10028
(212) 879-5655

Perinatal Loss
2116 N.E. 18th Avenue
Portland, OR 97212
(503) 284-7426

Contact each organization for a variety of publications relating to miscarriage, stillbirth, and early infant death, including the books *Still to Be Born* and *When Hello Means Good-bye.*

Index